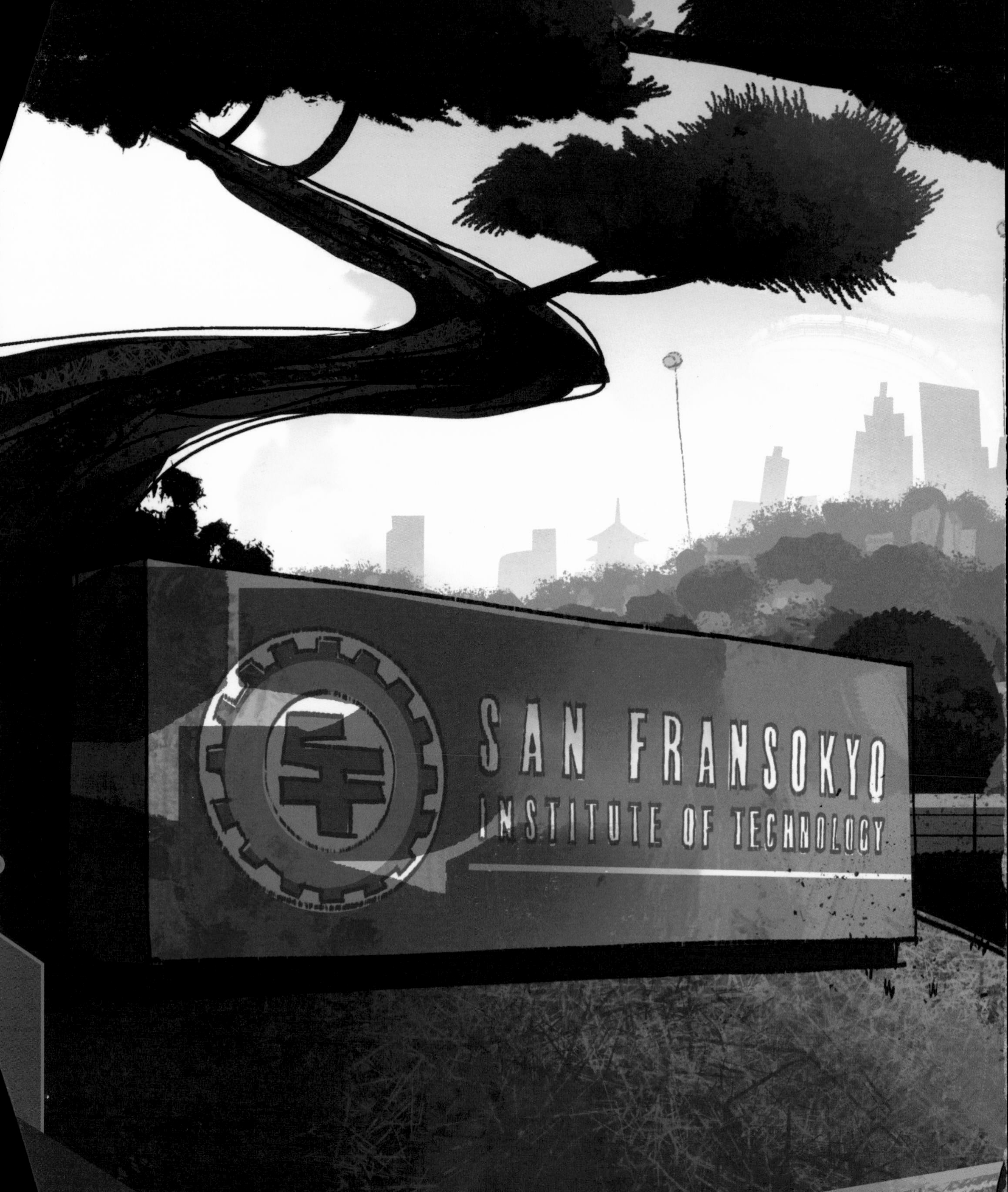
SAN FRANSOKYO
INSTITUTE OF TECHNOLOGY

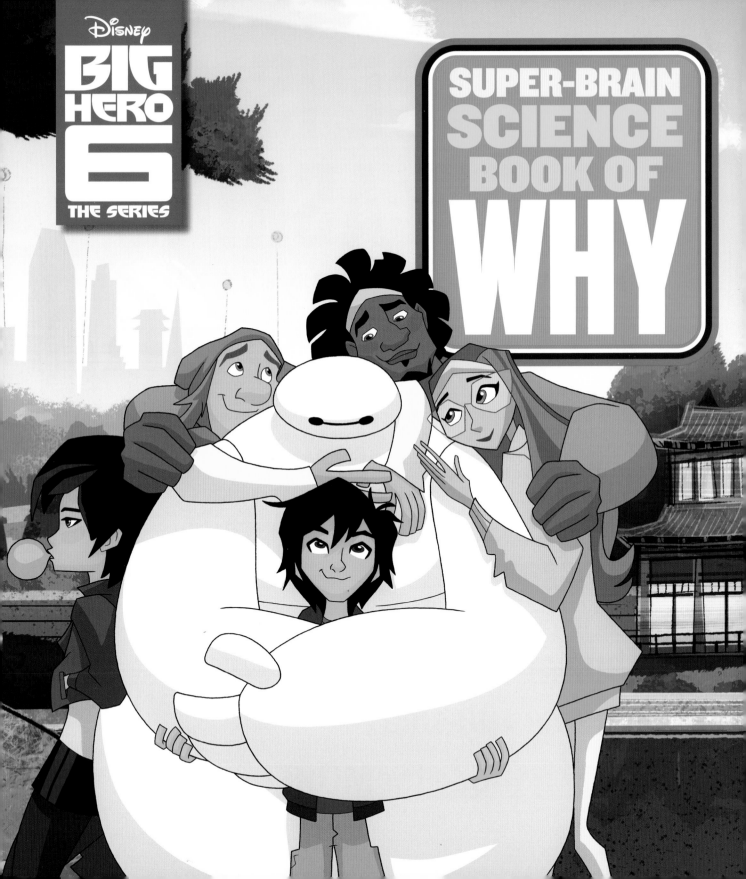

SCIENCE IS ALL ABOUT ASKING WHY... AND HOW!

The members of Big Hero 6 are super heroes with a serious appreciation for science. Understanding chemistry, engineering, technology and physics helps them build better robots, come up with new solutions and save San Fransokyo from bad guys. They want to understand questions like…

- **Why does baking soda and vinegar cause an explosion?**

- **Why is it so hard to make a humanoid robot?**

- **What is plasma?**

And a whole lot **MORE!**

TABLE OF CONTENTS

NO PROBLEM TOO BIG!

CRITICAL THINKING
Look for these questions and examples that help you sharpen your mind and analyze new information!

THE SCIENTIFIC METHOD

Science is all about asking questions, and then figuring out the answers—scientifically! The way we do that is through the scientific method.

サン　フランシスキョー

The word **SCIENCE** comes from the Latin word "scientia," which means knowledge!

STEP 1 ASK A QUESTION

The first step is deciding what you want to know, like why do some flowers turn toward the sun? What are fingernails for?
Does butter or oil make better chocolate chip cookies? Which battery is best for your robot? All of these questions (and so many more) have been figured out by scientists through research.

STEP 2 GATHER INFORMATION AND OBSERVE

One of the best ways to learn about something is to observe it. If you wanted to know how using butter or oil affects chocolate chip cookies, for example, you would spend a lot of time looking at butter and oil, notice things like their states of matter (butter is a solid, oil is a liquid) and their taste. You can also consider facts people have already recorded about butter and oil, like their different smoke points (the temperature at which each one begins to smoke) and how each is made.

STEP 3 FORM A HYPOTHESIS

Now that you've spent some time observing and thinking about butter and oil, you can make an educated guess about which one will make a better cookie. This educated guess is called a hypothesis. Write yours down!

サン フランシスキョー

Baking is chemistry, so ask yourself what Honey Lemon would think about this!

STEP 4 TEST YOUR HYPOTHESIS

Time to experiment! In this example, that also means it's time to make cookies.

When experimenting, you want to try to make sure everything is the same except what you're testing. That means both cookies should use the same exact recipe and be cooked for the same amount of time at the same temperature. Scientifically, you'd say that the flour, sugar, eggs, temperature and even the baking sheet are all constants, and the fat (butter or oil) is the variable. That way, you can be sure that whatever differences arise are because of the oil and butter, and nothing else.

WHEN EXPERIMENTING, YOU SHOULD USE SLOW, METHODICAL PRECISION, JUST LIKE WASABI WOULD.

WORDS TO KNOW
CONSTANT
A component of a scientific experiment that is always the same.
VARIABLE
A component of a scientific experiment that changes.

STEP 5 ANALYZE YOUR RESULTS

If you do this experiment, you'll see that the cookies look pretty much the same and have similar textures, but that the cookies made with oil are much greasier than the ones made with butter. Butter is the winner!

STEP 6 DRAW YOUR CONCLUSIONS

Now that you know that when you're making chocolate chip cookies, using butter is better than using the same amount of oil. But there are always more tests to be done. Do you think you'd get the same results in another cookie recipe? What about brownies?
What if you used less oil than butter?
There's only one way to find out!

You can try this experiment out for yourself—just use your favorite chocolate chip cookie recipe. Make it once as you usually do, and once again, swapping out the butter for the same amount of oil (weigh it to be sure). And don't forget to ask your parents for permission.

THE ANATOMY OF AN ATOM

The answer to a lot of scientific questions (especially those involving chemistry or physics) has to do with how different kinds of elements behave. Elements are all the different chemical substances scientists know about.

Humans have discovered 118 different elements. We organize them in something called a Periodic Table—you can look at one yourself on page 10. The smallest, single unit of an element is called an atom.

サン　フランソーキョー

Baymax's skeleton is made of carbon fiber. One carbon atom has 6 electrons.

WHAT IS AN ATOM?

Everything in the world is made up of atoms—think of it as the smallest possible unit of matter.
Every atom contains neutrons, protons and electrons. Neutrons and protons are in the center of the atom, and together they form a nucleus. Electrons spin very quickly around the nucleus, in layers called "shells." Electrons carry a negative charge, protons carry a positive charge and neutrons are neutral.

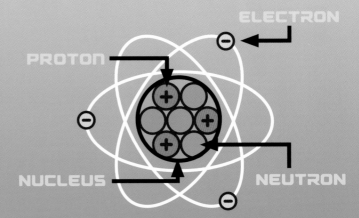

ELECTRON

PROTON

NUCLEUS

NEUTRON

ELECTRON SHELLS

An atom can have up to seven shells of electrons. Scientists refer to the shell closest to the nucleus as K. The next level is L, then M, N, O, P and Q.

Each shell can hold a different number of electrons. (K can hold 2, L can hold 8, M can hold 18, etc.) As the shells closer to the nucleus become filled, electrons will move out to a new shell. The outermost shell of an atom is called a valence shell.

Atoms always want to have a "full" valence shell. Knowing how many electrons are in each shell helps scientists understand how different elements will react when they meet one another. For example, hydrogen atoms only have one electron each (and therefore have a space to fill in their first shell). Oxygen atoms have eight electrons (and therefore have two spaces to fill in their second shells). So when two hydrogen atoms meet an oxygen atom, they bond to form H_2O—or as it's more commonly referred to, water!

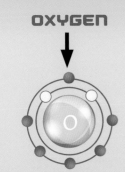

OXYGEN

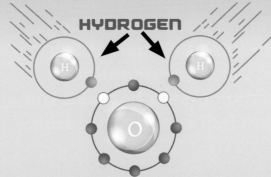

HYDROGEN

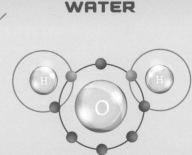

WATER

CHEMISTRY

Chemistry is the scientific study of substances and how substances interact with one another. With the help of chemistry, we can answer questions such as…

- ## Why do crystals form?

- ## Why do pancakes need baking powder?

- ## How do blow torches work?

MEET HONEY LEMON

Upbeat and quick-thinking, Honey Lemon is a chem major at the San Fransokyo Institute of Technology and an important member of Big Hero 6! She uses her chemistry smarts and mini purse to make the perfect chem ball for any situation.

WHY DOES MIXING BAKING SODA AND VINEGAR CAUSE AN EXPLOSION?

When Hiro attends Wendy Wower's Science Hour, she and Hiro show the kids (and Fred) how baking soda and vinegar combine to make an awesome explosion! But how exactly does that work?

The scientific name for baking soda is sodium bicarbonate. The name explains what the compound is made up of: one sodium atom, a hydrogen atom, an oxygen atom and a carbon dioxide molecule.

Vinegar is a mixture that contains, among other things, acetic acid. Acetic acid contains a hydrogen atom and an acetate ion.

When the acetic acid in vinegar meets sodium bicarbonate, a reaction occurs. The hydrogen in the acetic acid bonds with the hydrogen and oxygen to form a molecule of water (two hydrogens and one oxygen make H_2O)! Meanwhile, the acetate ion combines with the sodium atom to form a salt called sodium acetate. This frees the carbon dioxide from its previous bonds, so it bubbles up as a gas—that's the reaction you see!

WHY DO CHEMICAL REACTIONS HAPPEN?

A chemical reaction happens any time a set of substances undergoes a chemical change to make a different substance. Honey Lemon makes them happen whenever she uses her mini-purse, which is actually a mobile chemical lab. By selecting the right elements, she can make chem balls that create all sorts of reactions, from producing a cushiony foam to making smoke screens or freezing bad guys!

Chemical reactions aren't always that flashy, though. When you add baking powder to pancake batter (see page 20), that causes a chemical reaction! Your body also uses chemical reactions to break food down and turn it into energy. Rust forming on metal is another common example of a chemical reaction—when water is present, iron reacts with oxygen in the air, forming iron oxide. That's rust.

On a molecular level, chemical reactions occur when chemical bonds are broken or when new ones are made, creating a new molecule. Chemical bonds occur when atoms borrow or share electrons with other atoms in order to complete their outer shell.

WHAT'S THE DIFFERENCE BETWEEN A CHEMICAL REACTION AND A CHEMICAL SOLUTION?

If you combine water and sugar together and the sugar dissolves completely, is that a chemical reaction or a solution?

The answer is "solution," because the substances didn't really change—the molecules of sugar and water aren't affected. You could still separate the sugar from the water again by boiling the water, leaving the sugar behind.

But when you bake something, that is a chemical reaction because the substances have come together to make something totally different, and the molecules have changed. You can't unbake a cake and separate the ingredients again! Similarly, you can remove rust, but you can't turn it back into iron and oxygen.

WHY IS IT CALLED THE PERIODIC TABLE?

Honey Lemon, a chemistry major at San Fransokyo Institute of Technology, knows the periodic table like the back of her hand—or rather, the back of her purse! It's easy enough to follow once you understand how it's organized.

We call it the periodic table because the elements are lined up in rows called "periods." In each period, the elements are ordered according to their **atomic number**. All the elements in the first column have just 1 electron in their outer shell, and all the elements in the last column (known as the noble gases) have a full outer shell. The noble gases rarely react with other elements because of their full outer shells—they don't need any more electrons to be complete.

1 **H** HYDROGEN 1.0079											
3 **Li** LITHIUM 6.941	4 **Be** BERYLLIUM 9.0122										
11 **Na** SODIUM 22.989	12 **Mg** MAGNESIUM 24.305										
19 **K** POTASSIUM 39.098	20 **Ca** CALCIUM 40.078	21 **Sc** SCANDIUM 44.955	22 **Ti** TITANIUM 47.867	23 **V** VANADIUM 50.9415	24 **Cr** CHROMIUM 51.9961	25 **Mn** MANGANESE 54.938	26 **Fe** IRON 55.845	27 **Co** COBALT 58.933	28 **Ni** NICKEL 58.6934		
37 **Rb** RUBIDIUM 85.467	38 **Sr** STRONTIUM 87.62	39 **Y** YTTRIUM 88.9058	40 **Zr** ZICRONIUM 91.224	41 **Nb** NIOBIUM 92.9063	42 **Mo** MOLYBDENUM 95.95	43 **Tc** TECHNETIUM (98)	44 **Ru** RUTHENIUM 101.07	45 **Rh** RHODIUM 102.90	46 **Pd** PALLADIUM 106.42		
55 **Cs** CAESIUM 132.905	56 **Ba** BARIUM 137.327	57-71*	72 **Hf** HAFNIUM 178.49	73 **Ta** TANTALUM 180.94	74 **W** TUNGSTEN 183.84	75 **Re** RHENIUM 186.207	76 **Os** OSMIUM 190.23	77 **Ir** IRIDIUM 192.217	78 **Pt** PLATINUM 195.084		
87 **Fr** FRANCIUM (223)	88 **Ra** RADIUM (226)	89-103**	104 **Rf** RUTHERFORDIUM (267)	105 **Db** DUBNIUM (268)	106 **Sg** SEABORGIUM (271)	107 **Bh** BOHRIUM (272)	108 **Hs** HASSIUM (270)	109 **Mt** MEITNERIUM (276)	110 **Ds** DARMSTADT (281)		

57 **La** LANTHANUM 138.90	58 **Ce** CERIUM 140.116	59 **Pr** PRASEODYMIUM 140.90	60 **Nd** NEODYMIUM 144.242	61 **Pm** PROMETHIUM (145)	62 **Sm** SAMARIUM 150.36	63 **Eu** EUROPIUM 151.964	64 **Gd** GADOLI... 157.2
89 **Ac** ACTINIUM (227)	90 **Th** THORIUM 232.0377	90 **Pa** PROTACTINIUM 231.03	92 **U** URANIUM 238.02	93 **Np** NEPTUNIUM (237)	94 **Pu** PLUTONIUM (244)	95 **Am** AMERICIUM (243)	96 **Cm** CURIUM (247)

WORDS TO KNOW

ATOMIC NUMBER
The number of protons in a nucleus.

VALENCE ELECTRON
An outer shell electron that can form a chemical bond with another element if the outer shell is not already full.

You'll notice that sometimes rows skip a few columns—it was organized this way so that elements with the same number of **valence electrons** are grouped together in the same columns. Scientists did this because the number of **valence electrons** is an indicator of how an element will react in a certain situation.

| 2 He HELIUM 4.0026 |

| 5 B BORON 10.811 | 6 C CARBON 12.011 | 7 N NITROGEN 14.007 | 8 O OXYGEN 15.999 | 9 F FLUORINE 18.998 | 10 Ne NEON 20.1797 |

| 13 Al ALUMINIUM 26.981 | 14 Si SILICON 28.085 | 15 P PHOSPHORUS 30.974 | 16 S SULFUR 32.066 | 17 Cl CHLORINE 35.453 | 18 Ar ARGON 39.948 |

| Cu OPPER 3.546 | 30 Zn ZINC 65.38 | 31 Ga GALLIUM 69.723 | 32 Ge GERMANIUM 72.63 | 33 As ARSENIC 74.921 | 34 Se SELENIUM 78.971 | 35 Br BROMINE 79.904 | 36 Kr KRYPTON 83.798 |

| Ag ILVER 7.8682 | 48 Cd CADMIUM 112.414 | 49 In INDIUM 114.818 | 50 Sn TIN 118.710 | 51 Sb ANTIMONY 121.760 | 52 Te TELLURIUM 127.60 | 53 I IODINE 126.90 | 54 Xe XENON 131.293 |

| Au GOLD 96.96 | 80 Hg MERCURY 200.59 | 81 Tl THALLIUM 204.38 | 82 Pb LEAD 207.2 | 83 Bi BISMUTH 208.98 | 84 Po POLONIUM (209) | 85 At ASTATINE (210) | 86 Rn RADON (222) |

| Rg TGENIUM 280) | 112 Cn COPERNICIUM (285) | 113 Uut UNUNTRIUM (284) | 114 Fl FLEROVIUM (289) | 115 Uup UNUNPENTIUM (288) | 116 Lv LIVERMORIUM (293) | 117 Uus UNUNSEPTIUM (294) | 118 Uuo UNUNOCTIUM (294) |

| Tb RBIUM 58.92 | 66 Dy DYSPROSIUM 162.500 | 67 Ho HOLMIUM 164.93 | 68 Er ERBIUM 167.259 | 69 Tm THULIUM 168.93 | 70 Yb YTTERBIUM 173.054 | 71 Lu LUTETIUM 174.9668 |

| Bk KELIUM (247) | 98 Cf CALIFORNIUM (251) | 99 Es EINSTEINIUM (252) | 100 Fm FERMIUM (257) | 101 Md MENDELEVIUM (258) | 102 No NOBELIUM (259) | 103 Lr LAWRENCIUM (262) |

WATCH OUT FOR MY PITCH!

17

CHEMISTRY

WHY DO CHEMISTS HAVE SO MANY TOOLS?

When Honey Lemon is trying to create a compound that will stop Globby, she turns to her arsenal of chemistry supplies! Chemists need special equipment in order to carry out experiments. Everything needs to be carefully measured in order to achieve the same results each time.

1.

2.

3.

1. BUNSEN BURNER

Used to heat chemicals, a Bunsen burner is a small gas burner.

2. FLORENCE FLASK

Also known as a boiling flask, these flasks are used for heating liquids. The round bottom and long neck also makes it easy to swirl liquids in these flasks.

3. TEST TUBES

Used to hold small samples of liquids, test tubes make it easy to compare different liquids or the results of experiments.

4. TONGS

If a test tube is too hot or it's imperative to keep a good grip on something, a chemist may use tongs.

5. BALANCE

A balance is used to determine the mass of objects.

6. ERLENMEYER FLASK

Also known as a conical flask, the special shape of this flask makes it ideal for mixing chemicals with minimal risk of spilling.

7. BEAKERS

Beakers are used for mixing, stirring and heating chemicals. Beakers often have spouts to make pouring easier.

8. MORTAR & PESTLE

A mortar and pestle is used to grind chemicals into a fine powder, or crush solids into smaller pieces.

WHY DO PANCAKES NEED BAKING POWDER?

Fred wouldn't enjoy his victory pancakes as much if they didn't have baking powder! Baking powder contains baking soda and a powdered acid. Baking soda, a **basic** ingredient also known as sodium bicarbonate, is added to cakes (and other baked goods) to make them rise. The baking soda reacts with an **acidic**

WORDS TO KNOW

PH
A measure of hydrogen ion concentration.

ACIDIC
In chemistry, an acid is any substance with a pH of less than 7.

BASE
A base is any substance with a pH of more than 7.

WHY SHOULD PANCAKE BATTER BE LUMPY?

To understand this, first you need to understand gluten. Gluten is a protein in flour that's needed to give structure to pancakes and all kinds of baked goods. When flour gets wet, it activates the gluten molecules, making them loose and elastic. Mixing the wet flour lets the end of a gluten protein bond with the end of another gluten protein, "strengthening" it. So when you overmix pancake batter, it over-develops the gluten, which leads to sturdy (but not as delicious) pancakes. But if you mix the batter until "just combined," you'll wind up with elastic gluten—just right for giving the pancakes' structure while still allowing room for lots of air bubbles. Tasty!

ingredient, like lemon juice, milk, honey or brown sugar. When these two ingredients meet, they produce tiny bubbles of carbon dioxide that get trapped in the batter.

In the case of baking powder, the acid is already there—it just needs to meet something wet to start a chemical reaction!

WE CAUGHT A REVENGE-CRAZED VILLAIN, WE SAVED THE CITY, WE HAD VICTORY PANCAKES!

WHY IS TAPE STICKY?

WORDS TO KNOW

MOLECULE

A group of atoms bonded together. A molecule is the smallest unit of a chemical compound that can take part in a chemical reaction.

サン　フランシーキョー

When Baymax's exterior gets torn, Hiro knows just the thing for a quick fix—duct tape! But why, exactly, is tape so sticky? To understand this, first you need to understand what an ionic charge is. The ionic charge of a **molecule** is determined by the amount of electrons it has—if there are more electrons than protons, it has a negative charge. If there are fewer electrons than protons, it has a positive charge. (Remember, electrons are negative and protons are positive). If it has an equal number of electrons and protons, the ionic charge is neutral.

Tape is sticky because of these charges. Tape has an opposite ionic charge to most surfaces, making the two attract to one another.

HOW DO CRYSTALS FORM?

サン　フランシスキョー

WORDS TO KNOW

MAGMA
Hot, liquid rock.

MISSION FRIED RICE

BENITO'S

When Big Hero 6 tries to keep Globby from stealing a priceless piece of art, he turns some of his "Globbyness" into crystals, tripping Go Go. Of course, this isn't how crystals usually form in nature!

Crystals form via a process called crystallization, and this can happen in a few different ways.

Traditional crystals, like diamonds, rubies and emeralds, often form when **magma** cools slowly. As the **magma** cools, molecules in the liquid gather together in a repeating pattern, forming the crystal.

Other examples of crystallization are snowflakes (ice crystals) and salt crystals, which form when salt water evaporates.

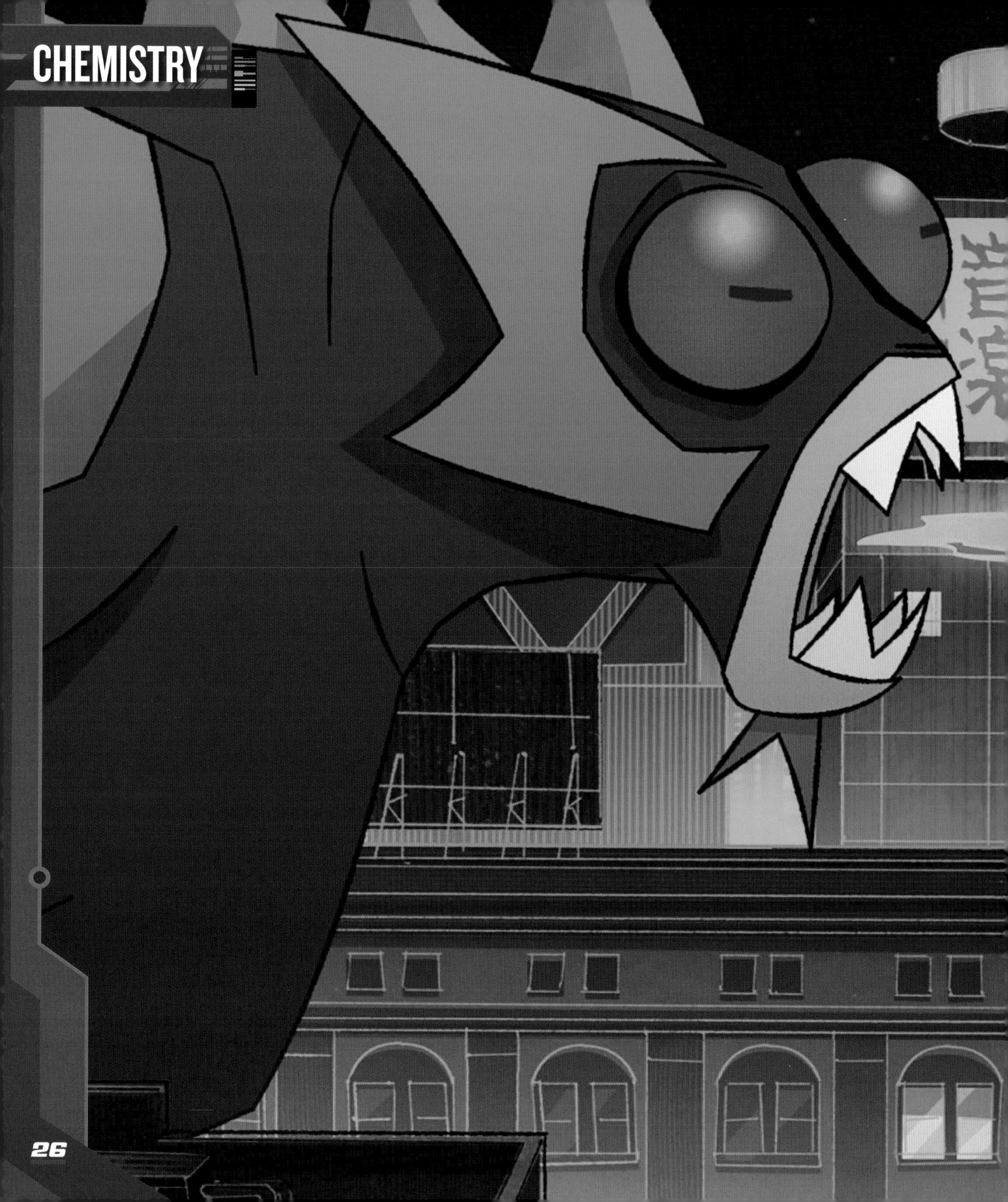

WHY DOES FIRE NEED OXYGEN?

When Fred makes his dream of a life sized, fire breathing kaiju come to life, he comes to regret it pretty quickly! The kaiju can breathe fire for a couple of reasons. For one thing, Fred was going for accuracy. But because the kaiju was also outside in the open air, where plenty of oxygen was available.

Fires need three things: Fuel, heat and an oxygen content of at least 16 percent. The air we breathe is 21 percent oxygen. When fuel meets heat and oxygen, the resulting chemical reaction is what creates fire.

GUYS, SORRY I INADVERTENTLY CREATED A MONSTER THAT ALMOST DESTROYED THE CITY!

WHY DOES SOAP FORM BUBBLES?

As Baymax learns in the children's science museum, soap bubbles are fascinating! They form when water meets soap—but why?

A soap bubble is technically a thin layer of water surrounded by soap molecules. One end of a soap molecule attracts water, while the other end repels it. So when soap comes in contact with water, the soap molecules surround the water, with the attracting ends facing inward and the repellant ends facing outward.

WHY IS ICE SLIPPERY?

When Big Hero 6 needs to quickly get to action, Honey Lemon creates a slide made of ice! It's a smart choice because the slide is so slippery.

Interestingly, the ice itself isn't slippery—there's a very thin layer of water on top of ice, making it wet. And as anyone who has ever ignored a "CAUTION WET FLOOR" sign knows, wet things are slippery!

What's even more interesting is that scientists aren't exactly sure why there's a thin layer of water on top of ice. One simple theory is that as soon as someone steps on ice, the heat from the friction is just enough to melt a very thin layer. Another theory is that ice inherently has a liquid layer because its surface molecules have nothing above them to bind to.

HOW DO BLOW TORCHES WORK?

Thanks in part to her blow torch, Aunt Cass really brought the heat in Food Fight, an underground cooking competition!

Blow torches are really just self-contained fire makers. Like any fire, they combine a **combustible** (gas) with oxygen (either from the air around it, or to make an extra-oxidized fire, with added oxygen from a tank) and set off the reaction with an igniter.

Blow torches can be adjusted to make flames that are hotter or cooler. By using a gas with a very high burning point and adding a lot of oxygen, you can produce a fire that can melt metal! Most kitchen torches use butane, a cooler burning gas—it doesn't take nearly as much heat to caramelize sugar as it does to **weld** metal.

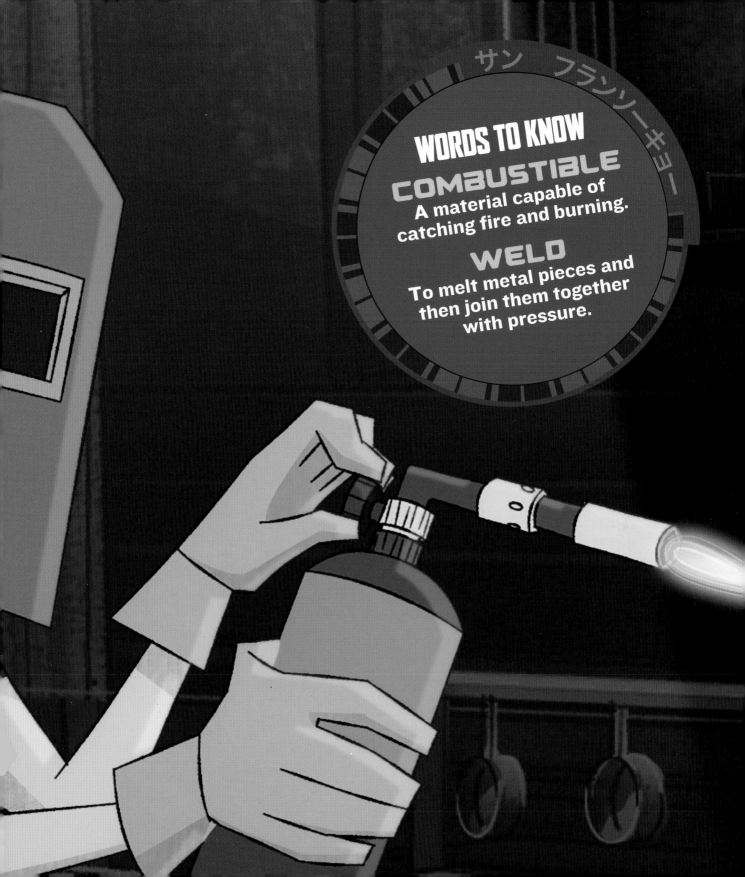

サン　フランシスキョー

WORDS TO KNOW

COMBUSTIBLE
A material capable of catching fire and burning.

WELD
To melt metal pieces and then join them together with pressure.

HOW DO SCRATCH AND SNIFF STICKERS WORK?

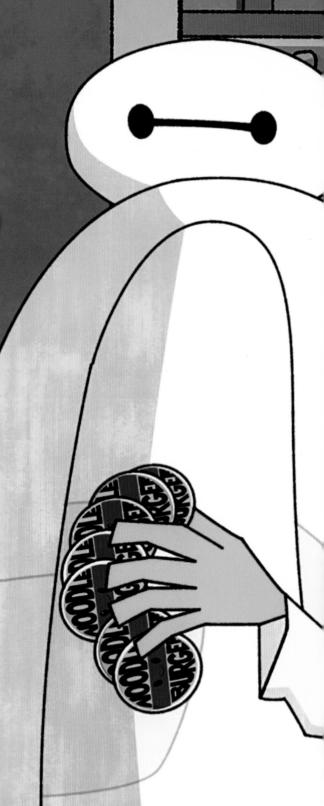

Before Noodle Burger Boy became a villain, one of his favorite things to do was give out scratch and sniff stickers—and boy did Fred love smelling them!

Scratch and sniff stickers work for an incredibly long time. This is because of their design. A scratch and sniff sticker uses something called microencapsulation technology. Basically, tiny bits of an aroma-generating chemical (like perfume) are contained in tiny plastic spheres that are just a few **microns** in diameter. When you scratch the sticker, you break some of these spheres, releasing the smell of candy, flowers or greasy but delicious burgers.

WORDS TO KNOW

MICRON

Also known as a micrometer, a micron is a measurement of length one thousandth of a millimeter. One millimeter is equal to .I centimeters, or about .03 inches.

TECHNOLOGY

Technology encompasses all sort of inventions. Most recent technology stems from computer science. Innovations in technology have enabled humans to invent robots, visit outer space and more! When we consider technology, we can ask questions such as...

- ## Why are computer chips so important?

- ## Why is it so difficult to make a humanoid robot?

- ## How do 3-D scanners work?

MEET HIRO

A boy genius and the youngest student ever at the San Fransokyo Institute of Technology, Hiro is fascinated by all things having to do with robots. He's also a key member of Big Hero 6! Together with Baymax, Hiro uses his brain and knowledge of technology to help save the day.

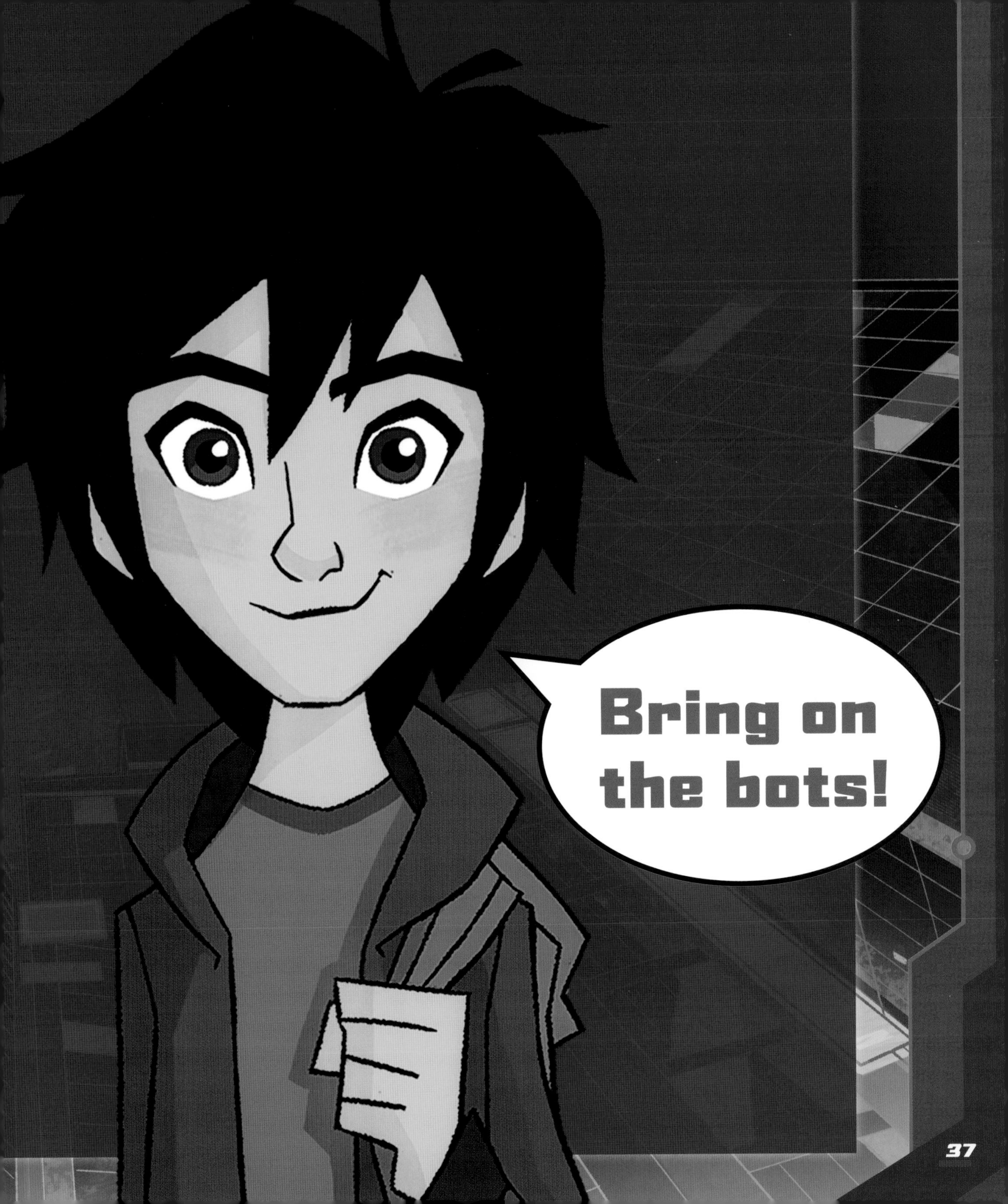
Bring on the bots!

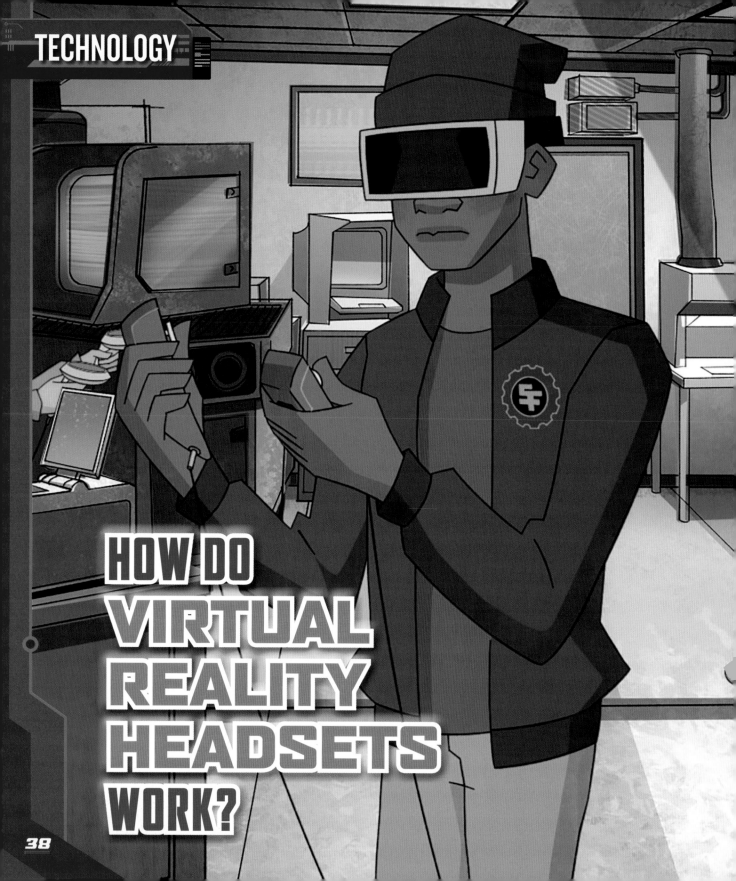

HOW DO VIRTUAL REALITY HEADSETS WORK?

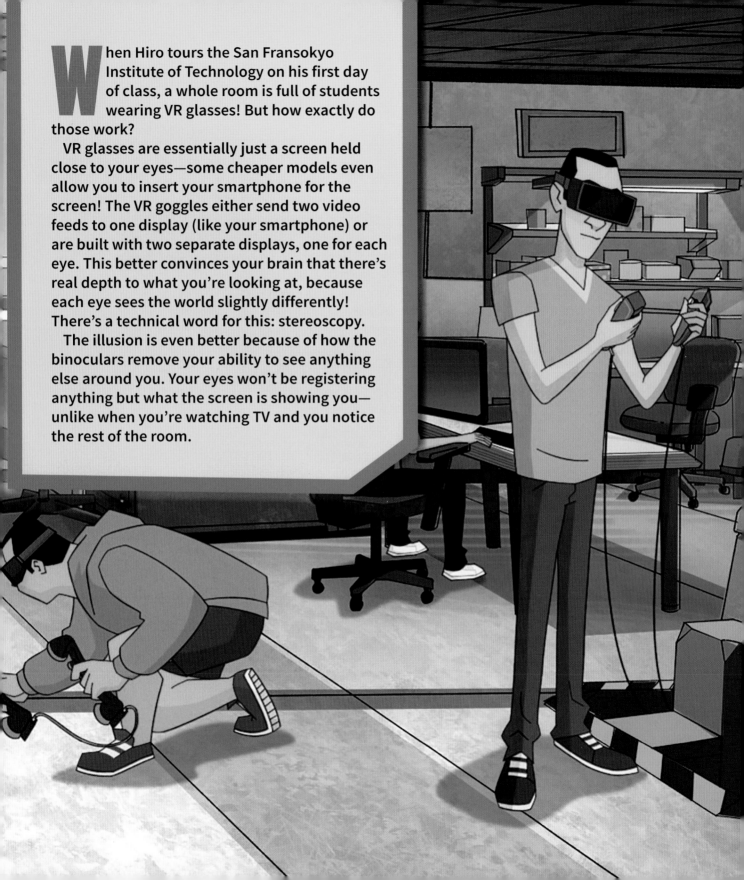

When Hiro tours the San Fransokyo Institute of Technology on his first day of class, a whole room is full of students wearing VR glasses! But how exactly do those work?

VR glasses are essentially just a screen held close to your eyes—some cheaper models even allow you to insert your smartphone for the screen! The VR goggles either send two video feeds to one display (like your smartphone) or are built with two separate displays, one for each eye. This better convinces your brain that there's real depth to what you're looking at, because each eye sees the world slightly differently! There's a technical word for this: stereoscopy.

The illusion is even better because of how the binoculars remove your ability to see anything else around you. Your eyes won't be registering anything but what the screen is showing you—unlike when you're watching TV and you notice the rest of the room.

WHY DID WE INVENT ROBOTS?

The word robot comes from the Czech word "robota," which means "forced labor." Basically, robots were invented to do things that are very difficult, dangerous or tedious for humans to do. For example, Noodle Burger Boy was invented to be entertaining and carry out simple tasks, like taking orders for sandwiches with way too many pickles, but was soon reprogrammed to do some pretty unhelpful things!

WHY IS IT SO DIFFICULT TO MAKE A HUMANOID ROBOT?

Building a robot that walks on two feet and moves like a human is really hard! That's one of the reasons it took Tadashi such a long time to put together Baymax, and that's without even considering all of his healthcare capabilities. It's also one of the reasons Hiro shouldn't have skipped the diagnostics test after he put Baymax together—a lot of things can go wrong.

But why is it so hard? Humans have upwards of 21 senses (not just 5). Our senses of balance, proprioception (knowing where your body parts are in relation to one another) and kinesthetic sense (knowing how to move your body parts in relation to one another) are all very difficult things to code—and tough for a robot to learn how to do! Inventors challenge themselves with events like the RoboCup, a soccer game played entirely by robots! The robots aren't yet as good as humans—in the 2017 games, they often moved slowly and were easily turned around. But the founders of the game have a goal: By 2050, they want to create a robot team that can beat human World Cup champions. Good luck, bots!

I AM NOT FAST.

WHY DO VACUUM ROBOTS KNOW WHERE MESSES ARE?

If a student spills a drink in SFIT's dining hall, it's no big deal—the mop bots will clean it up! Vacuum robots mostly move around randomly, though more advanced models will "map" a room and clean it in a more organized fashion. But thanks to piezoelectric sensors, vacuum robots know when they've hit an especially dirty area.

Piezoelectric sensors are basically crystals (like quartz) that generate electric pulses when something strikes them. (If you've ever owned a quartz watch, you can thank piezoelectricity for telling you what time it is!) When the vacuum robot runs over a lot of dirt, this triggers the piezoelectric sensor, and the bot knows to go over that same spot again until it's clean.

WHY IS IT IMPORTANT TO RUN COMPUTER DIAGNOSTICS?

WORDS TO KNOW

BACK UP
Archive computer data so it may be restored in the event of a crash.

VIRUS
A computer code that is capable of copying itself and does damage to a computer system or its files.

MY BODY HAS RUN AWAY.

This is a lesson that Hiro found out the hard way. Impatient to finish rebuilding Baymax, he skipped running the diagnostic program and booted up his robot anyway, only to have the body trash his lab and run away!

What exactly do diagnostics do for your computer, though? Well, they diagnose, or determine, any problems it might have. And it's always better to know about a problem before it gets worse. Diagnostics tests will scan your computer for **viruses**, clear out unwanted files that are slowing down your computer, **back up** important files so you don't lose them and help keep your files secure and private.

HOW DOES GPS WORK?

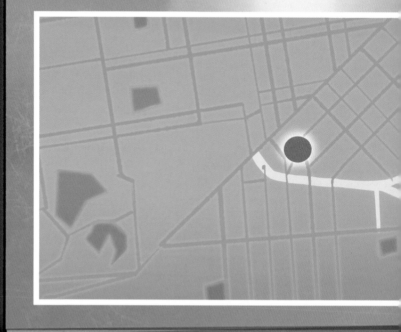

サン　フランシーキョー

WORDS TO KNOW

TRILATERATION
The process of figuring out a location by using geometry.

When Hiro and Fred go to Good Luck Alley, Baymax can easily show Honey Lemon, Wasabi and Go Go where they are thanks to his GPS!

GPS stands for Global Positioning System. There are about 30 satellites orbiting around Earth, all transmitting information about where they are at each moment.

No matter where you are on Earth, at least four GPS satellites are within your line of sight (even if you can't actually see them). Your GPS receiver intercepts the information from the GPS satellites closest to you, which it then uses to figure out your location using a process called **trilateration.**

Trilateration works like this: If your GPS knows you are X miles from Satellite A, it still doesn't know exactly where you are—there are a lot of locations that are X miles from Satellite A. But using similar data from two more satellites, it can pinpoint the one spot where you are simultaneously X miles from Satellite A, Y miles from Satellite B and Z miles from Satellite C.

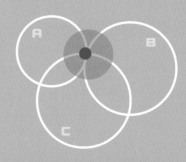

> HIRO CAN BE FOUND HERE.

FACTS ABOUT SATELLITES

Satellites are objects that scientists send into space so they can send information back to earth. They're usually launched by rockets—the first one, called *Sputnik*, was launched in 1957.

There are three main kinds of satellites: Those used for GPS services, those dedicated to handling voice, data and video transmissions, and scientific research satellites used for projects like transmitting meteorological data and taking pictures of Earth or other parts of the universe to send back to scientists.

WHY ARE COMPUTER CHIPS SO IMPORTANT?

Hiro thought Baymax was gone forever, until he found his computer chip in the robot's fist. Computer chips are like the brain of a computer—once Hiro had that, he just needed to build Baymax a new body!

Computer chips, also called integrated circuits, revolutionized computer technology. Before they were invented, the components needed for computers to store information and run programs took up entire rooms. Computer chips are a way of compressing all those components so that a computer can store a lot of information without taking up a lot of space. Computer chips made it possible to create everything from digital watches to computerized rockets to incredible robots!

WHAT ARE THE COMPONENTS OF THE CENTRAL PROCESSING UNIT?

Whenever Hiro needs Baymax to learn something new, whether it's how to be a superhero or teach Fred to dance, all he has to do is write computer code for Baymax.

Computers do all the incredible things they do because they are following instructions written by programmers like Hiro. The part of the computer that executes the code containing these instructions is called the central processing unit, or CPU.

The CPU is made up of electronic circuit parts:

 RESISTOR A device that limits the passage of electricity.

 CAPACITOR A component that stores electricity.

 DIODE A computer part that only allows electricity to flow in one direction.

 TRANSISTOR An electronic switch that can turn power off and on.

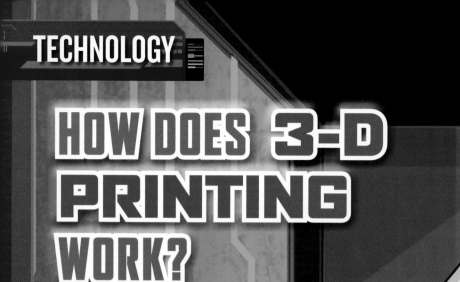

HOW DOES 3-D PRINTING WORK?

Every time Hiro needs to make new armor for Baymax he just puts the specifications in his 3-D printer, and soon enough, it's ready to go! 3-D printers work a lot like regular printers, except they can print in just about any material. They continue to print over the same space, allowing the printer to build a 3-D object, one very thin layer at a time. Incredibly, 3-D printers can make just about anything, as long as someone can design it! 3-D printers can make anything from everyday objects like coasters and shelves to much more complex objects, like working cars and prosthetic limbs.

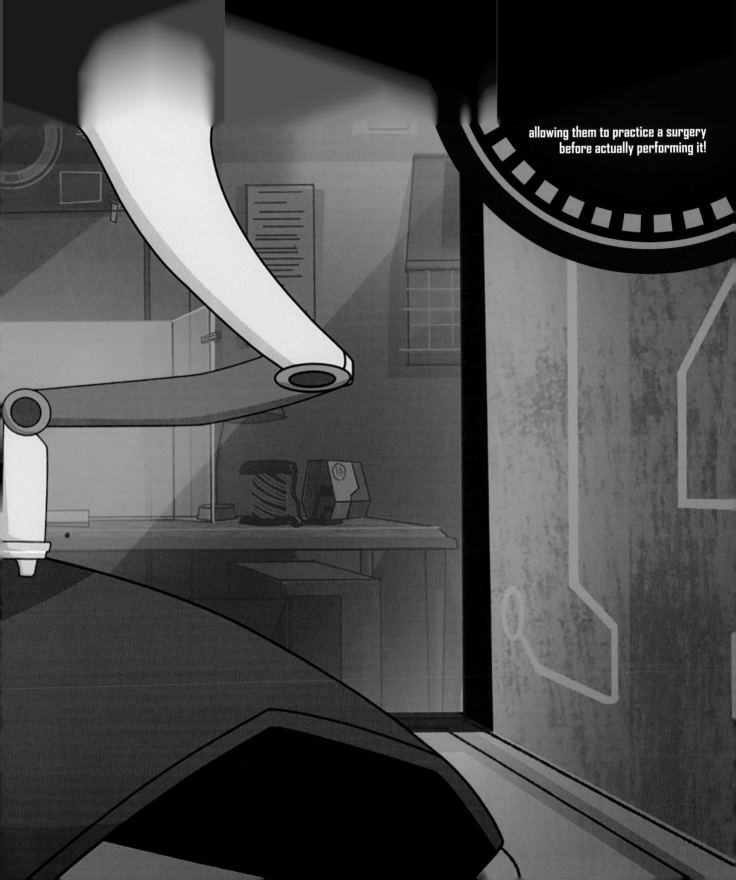

HOW DO 3-D SCANNERS WORK?

When Hiro needed to find Professor Granville's paperweight before any of Yama's bots get to it, he had Baymax use his scanner to locate the object immediately.

First, the scanner acquires data about the object. It does this using both a laser probe and cameras. As the laser projects a light onto an object, the cameras record how the distance and shape of the light changes. This information is sent back to a computer as millions of data points, collectively known as a "point cloud." Then the computer merges all of this information into a digital representation of whatever's being scanned.

WAIT. YOU GUYS REALLY THOUGHT IT WAS A PAPERWIGHT? WHATEVER THE VILLAIN'S TRYING TO GET IS NEVER WHAT IT SEEMS> THAT'S COMIC BOOK 101.

WHY CAN SOME BATTERIES BE RECHARGED?

If Baymax is acting sluggish and saying strange things, it's probably because his battery is running low! Thankfully, he can recharge his battery.

Batteries, whether rechargeable or not, produce power by an electrochemical reaction (see more about this below!). With regular batteries, once the initial charge runs out, the battery has died and is no longer usable. Rechargeable batteries, however, can reverse the reaction that occurs. Because of this, when rechargeable batteries receive energy from an outside source, it restores the battery's charge.

HOW DO BATTERIES WORK?

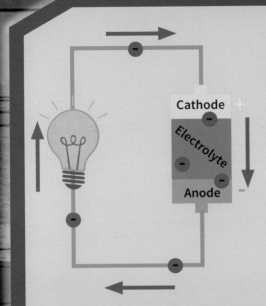

A battery is made up of power units called cells. It contains two electrical terminals, or electrodes, called a cathode and an anode. Between the electrodes is a chemical called an electrolyte.

When a battery is connected to a circuit (this happens whenever you are using it), it activates the electrolyte. The electrolyte reacts with the electrodes, creating an excess of electrons, which are used to power whatever the battery is connected to. When the electrolyte's reaction is finally finished, the battery has "died."

NO SERVICE

サン　フランシスコ

WORDS TO KNOW

DEAD ZONE

An area where phones and computers can't get a signal.

WHY DO CELLULAR DEAD ZONES OCCUR?

When Go Go, Honey Lemon and Wasabi go looking for Fred, Hiro and Baymax in Muirahara Woods, Go Go eventually notices something strange—the whole area is a dead zone! In the case of Muirahara Woods, this is because "Bessie," a meteorite, struck the area. The magnetic field given off by Bessie "kills" all the tech in the area (and makes Baymax act pretty odd). However, most magnets aren't nearly as strong as Bessie—you don't have to worry about a refrigerator magnet affecting your tech. But you might find yourself in a "dead zone" because something is blocking your cell phone's signal. Cell phones get their signal from towers that send out the signal to your phone. Dead zones are usually places that have something standing between the nearest cell tower and your cell phone. Bad weather, like thunderstorms, can also affect your phone's signal connection, as the harsh weather conditions can disrupt the signal that is being sent from the cell tower.

ON A SCALE OF ONE TO 10, HOW WOULD YOU RATE YOUR PINEAPPLE?

WHY DO PEOPLE WEAR SMART FABRIC AND OTHER TECHNOLOGY?

Wearable technology like Hiro's smart fabric can do some pretty neat things. Hiro invented a fabric that constricted his muscles to make him super strong. It admittedly had some drawbacks, but it was also pretty awesome!

Most smart fabrics and wearable technology currently on the market are not quite as advanced as what Hiro invented, but people do wear "smart" fabrics and wristbands so they can learn more about their bodies. Some athletes wear T-shirts that have a ton of tiny sensors in them that track their heart-rate, their steps and how deeply they breathe. Many people who enjoy exercising wear tiny computers on their wrists, often called smart watches. This tech is capable of tracking how far they've walked, how many calories they've burned and how well they've slept.

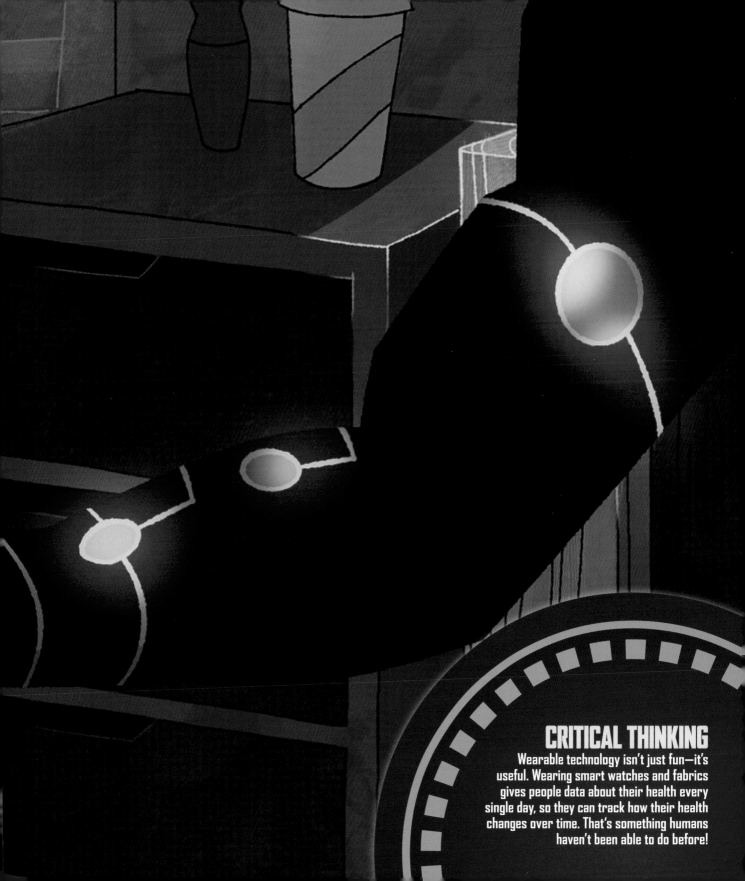

CRITICAL THINKING

Wearable technology isn't just fun—it's useful. Wearing smart watches and fabrics gives people data about their health every single day, so they can track how their health changes over time. That's something humans haven't been able to do before!

ENGINEERING

Engineering has to do with the design, building, and use of engines, machines and structures. Thanks to engineers, we've been able to do things like invent cars, build skyscrapers and even travel to space! When you're learning about engineering, you might have questions like...

- Why do cars have **hydraulic breaks?**
- Why do **X-rays** only show bones?
- How do **space rockets** launch?

MEET GO GO

An incredibly talented mechanical engineering student at SFIT, Go Go can seem rather tough until you get to know her. From her quick wit to her even quicker maglev discs, Go Go loves everything fast—combined with her engineering abilities and athletic skills, she's another valuable member of Big Hero 6.

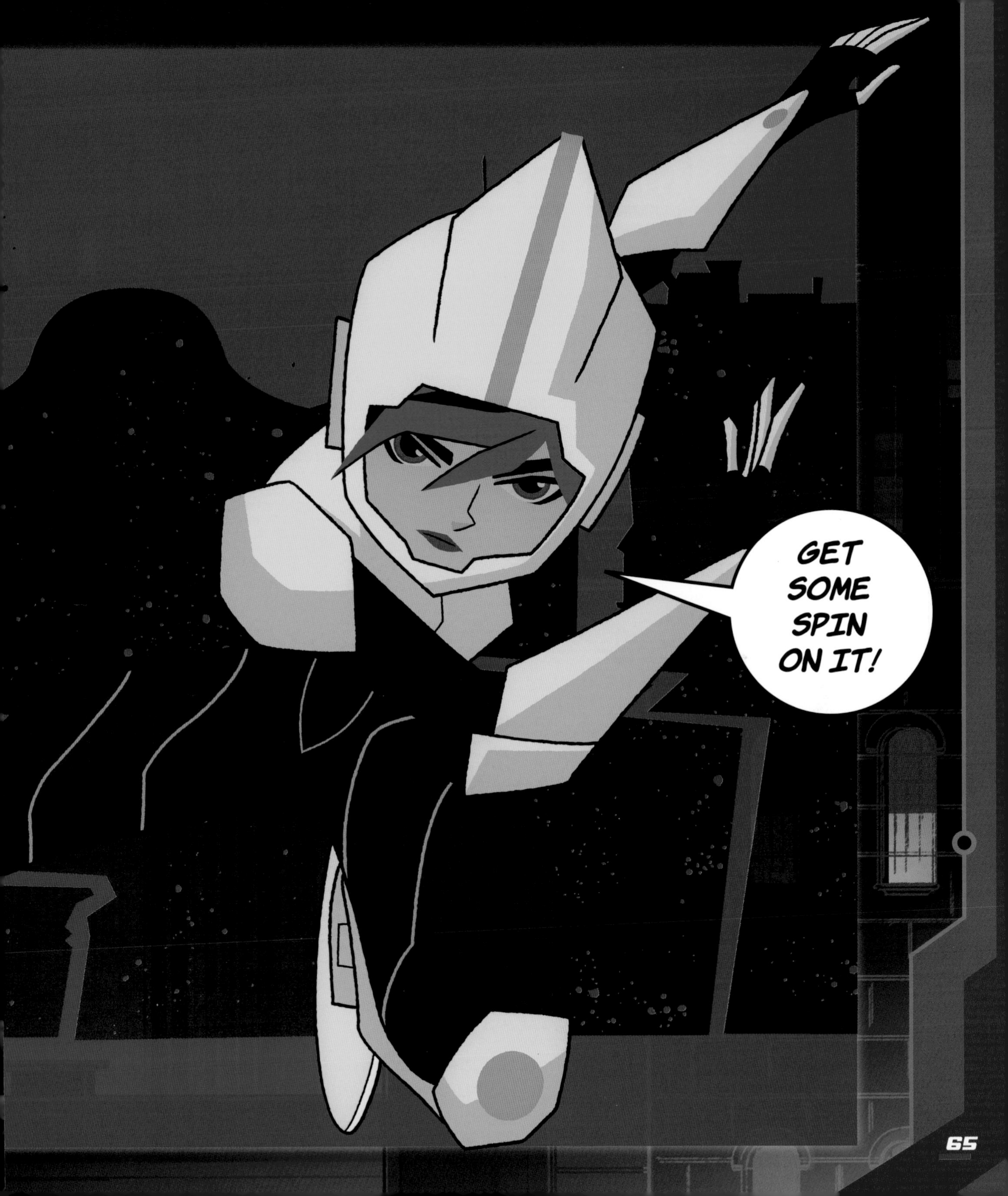
GET SOME SPIN ON IT!

WHY DO BIKES HAVE DIFFERENT GEARS?

Changing gears changes how far you go with every turn of the pedal, and switching gears while riding a bike will help you ride more easily on different types of terrain. High gears are best for riding downhill or at high speeds; low gears will help you pedal up a hill.

SPROCKET
Also known as cogs, these are attached to the middle of the rear wheel and look like smaller versions of the chainring. Most bikes have 8-11 sprockets.

GEAR CABLE
Attached to the derailleurs, these let the rider shift gear by adjusting shifters located next to the handles.

DERAILLEURS
The derailleurs move the chain between the different sprockets and chainrings.

CHAIN
The chain is attached between the chainring and the chosen sprocket.

CHAINRING
This is the ring attached to the pedal, which in turn pulls the chain.

HOW DO THEY WORK?
When the rider adjusts the gear shifter, it either shortens or lengthens the gear cable. This causes the derailleur to move into a new position on the chainring or sprocket, effectively shortening or lengthening the chain. As the rider pedals, the chainring turns the chain and the chain turns the axle connected to the back wheel.

WHY DON'T WE EVER FORGET HOW TO RIDE A BIKE?

CRITICAL THINKING
Scientists are excited about the Aberdeen nerve cell discovery because it could be helpful in developing prosthetic devices that can better carry out regular brain functions. Can you think of any other benefits to better understanding how our brains memorize motor functions?

Hiro was nervous when Tadashi was teaching him how to ride a bike. But now that he knows how, he never needs to be nervous again—knowing how to ride a bike isn't something you ever forget! But why is that?

According to **neuroscientists** at the University of Aberdeen in Scotland, a certain type of nerve cell in your **cerebellum** is responsible for remembering all sorts of motor skills, from using chopsticks to riding a bike!

WORDS TO KNOW

CEREBELLUM
A part of the brain responsible for coordinating and regulating muscle activity.

NEUROSCIENTIST
A scientist with specialized knowledge of the nervous system, including the brain, spinal cord and nerve cells.

WHY DO CARS HAVE HYDRAULIC BRAKES?

When Fred, Hiro and Baymax want to know where Go Go is going, they follow her in Fred's limousine. Baymax almost gives them away by waving when they're both stopped at a red light—it's a close call!

Of course, there would be a lot more close calls at red lights if it weren't for hydraulic brakes! It takes a lot of force to stop a moving car—a lot more than just pressing down on a pedal with your foot. But using hydraulic brakes multiplies the force from that pedal, which slows down and stops the car.

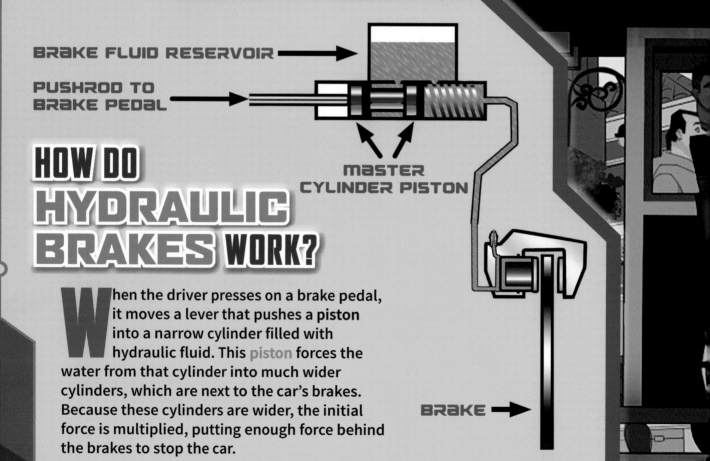

BRAKE FLUID RESERVOIR

PUSHROD TO BRAKE PEDAL

MASTER CYLINDER PISTON

BRAKE

HOW DO HYDRAULIC BRAKES WORK?

When the driver presses on a brake pedal, it moves a lever that pushes a **piston** into a narrow cylinder filled with hydraulic fluid. This **piston** forces the water from that cylinder into much wider cylinders, which are next to the car's brakes. Because these cylinders are wider, the initial force is multiplied, putting enough force behind the brakes to stop the car.

WORDS TO KNOW
PISTON

A piston is a disk or short cylinder that fits snugly within a tube. Pistons move up and down against a gas or liquid.

WHY DO SKYSCRAPERS SWAY?

Each year, first year students at SFIT are assigned the same project: to design a skyscraper that can withstand an earthquake that reaches 9.0 on the Richter scale. Karmi's design allows her skyscraper to sway with the tremors.

Virtually every tall building—from the Empire State Building to the Pyramids—sways when it's windy. For most buildings the swaying is hardly noticeable, but as buildings get taller, they become more affected by the wind. A little bit of swaying is good: If the buildings stayed completely rigid, the pressure of the wind could damage the building. But if the building sways too much, the people inside the building are likely to feel nauseated.

To prevent this, engineers have come up with some clever solutions: Some skyscrapers have tuned mass dampers, which counteract the swaying. Other buildings, like China's Shanghai World Financial Center, are designed with holes to let the wind flow through.

WORDS TO KNOW

TUNED MASS DAMPER

A TMD is a vibrating mass that counteracts the motion of the structure to which it is suspended.

サン　フランシスキョー

MY PROTOTYPE USES NICKEL TITANIUM AS A SHAPE MEMORY ALLOY, WHICH ALLOWS IT TO HAVE INCREASED PLASTICITY UNDER PRESSURE.

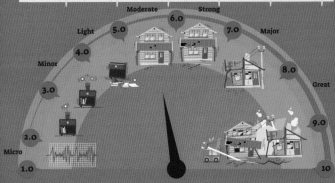

THE RICHTER SCALE

Moderate   Strong

Light 5.0   6.0   7.0   Major

4.0

Minor

3.0   8.0

Great

2.0   9.0

Micro

1.0   10

Invented in 1934 by California scientist Charles Richter, the Richter scale is used to classify earthquakes based on readings from a seismograph. Most earthquakes that happen register as 2.5 or less—these are too small to be felt by people. Up to 30,000 minor to moderate earthquakes happen each year, while great earthquak...

WORDS TO KNOW

RADIATION

Radiation is the release of energy as electromagnetic waves.

サン　フランシスコ

WHY DO X-RAYS ONLY SHOW YOUR BONES?

After Hiro takes on the Mad Jacks by himself, an X-ray reveals that he has fractured his leg. (Though actually, as Baymax points out, Hiro's leg is fractured in two places.) X-rays are a form of radiation. When an X-ray is taken, the radiation travels in waves. Radiation can pass through most objects, though different parts of the body will absorb the X-rays in different amounts. Bones, which are dense, absorb much more radiation than fat, muscle or organs. Because of this, bones show up white on an X-ray, while the rest of the body shows up in shades of gray.

IT'S OUTRAGEOUS! TO SNEAK OUTSIDE IN YOUR CONDITION TO CHASE DOWN FLYING DAREDEVILS... AND NOT CALL ME. THERE ARE NO WORDS.

WHY DO CRANES USE ELECTROMAGNETS?

While Hiro and Wasabi are busy arguing with each other, Noodle Burger Boy uses a crane to pick up Baymax!

The crane that picks up Baymax is a traditional one. If Baymax were a lot heavier, it wouldn't have been able to lift him. When cranes need to lift something extremely heavy, they often use electromagnets. Electromagnets have a soft iron core and electrically conducting wire. By adding an electric current, engineers have made electromagnets a lot stronger than any natural magnet. A regular magnet wouldn't be able to pick up a whole car, but an electromagnet can! That makes it perfect to use for a crane in a junkyard.

CRITICAL THINKING

Having a super strong magnet could cause problems—how would you move a magnet that strong without accidentally attracting big pieces of steel, like cars? Engineers solved this problem by making it so the electrical current that increases the force of an electromagnet can be turned on and off, giving crane operators control over how strong the magnet is at any given time.

HOW DO SPACE ROCKETS LAUNCH?

When Mochi's "slow clap" video edges out Mr. Sparkles's as the most-watched video on the internet, Mr. Sparkles gets very jealous. He kidnaps Mochi, puts him in a rocket and tries to make him a real star! Thankfully, Hiro saves Mochi before he makes it to outer space.

Though rockets are difficult to design and a lot of work goes into making sure a rocket is on the right trajectory, the main concept of how a rocket takes off is fairly simple. Rocket engines burn fuel, which turns the fuel into hot gas. The gas is pushed out of the bottom of the rocket, as exhaust. This causes the rocket to move in the opposite direction. This result is explained by Newton's Third Law of Motion (see more on page 125).

CRITICAL THINKING

You might be wondering why space shuttles don't just use the same engines that cars and planes do. Both plane and car engines need air in order to work— but there's no air in space! Because of this, space shuttles use rocket engines, which don't need any air to function.

HUMAN BIOLOGY

Biology is the study of living organisms. Human biology is a field of biology that focuses on (you guessed it!) humans. Studying humans in this way helps us better understand how our bodies work, how to treat illnesses and how to live the healthiest lives we can.
When you're studying human biology, you might ask questions like...

- ## How does your brain control your body?

- ## Why do hugs make people feel better?

- ## Why do people need sleep?

MEET BAYMAX

Baymax is a robot and a personal healthcare companion. Invented by Tadashi Hamada, Baymax is innocent, huggable and programmed to care for people. But thanks to a few upgrades from Hiro, Baymax is also a crime-fighting member of Big Hero 6!

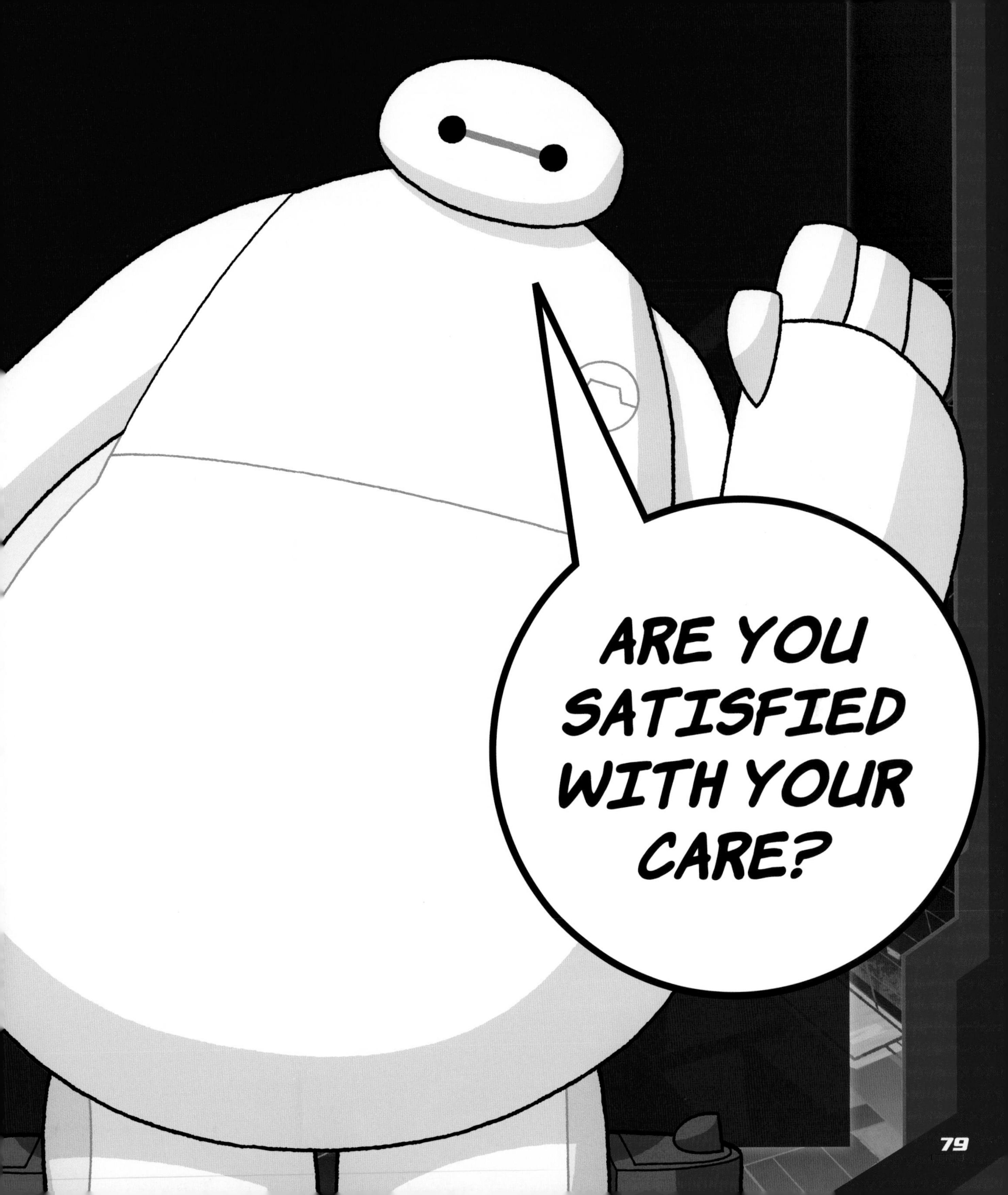
ARE YOU SATISFIED WITH YOUR CARE?

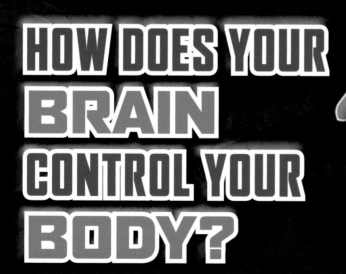

HOW DOES YOUR BRAIN CONTROL YOUR BODY?

When Dibs steals Honey Lemon's mini purse, he gets more than he bargained for! One of her chem balls seems to permanently attach Krei's neurotransmitter technology to his head, turning him into Globby. Eventually Globby realizes he can make his new body turn into anything, just by thinking about it.

While humans can't change their chemical makeup with their minds, it is still pretty incredible how our brains are in charge of everything our bodies do! From keeping your heart beating to riding a skateboard, absolutely everything your body does is controlled by your brain.

Your brain is the main component of something called the nervous system. Together with the spinal cord and a network of nerves that spans throughout the entire body, the nervous system helps the brain communicate with the rest of the body.

There are two main sets of nerves. One set, known as the autonomic nervous system, is automatic. These nerves convey information for things like releasing enzymes, breathing and sweating. The other set is known as the somatic nervous system. Those nerves are the ones that control stuff you have to think about in order to do, like walking or moving your fingers.

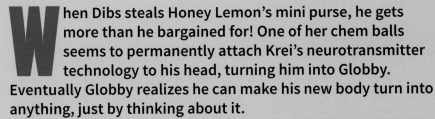

BRAIN

SPINAL CORD

NERVES

CRITICAL THINKING

Sometimes your body does move without your brain telling it to—out of reflex! You might move your hand away from something hot or blink when something is coming toward your face before your brain has even processed what's happening. Why do you think our bodies do things like this?

WHY DOES ADRENALINE MAKE PEOPLE BRAVE?

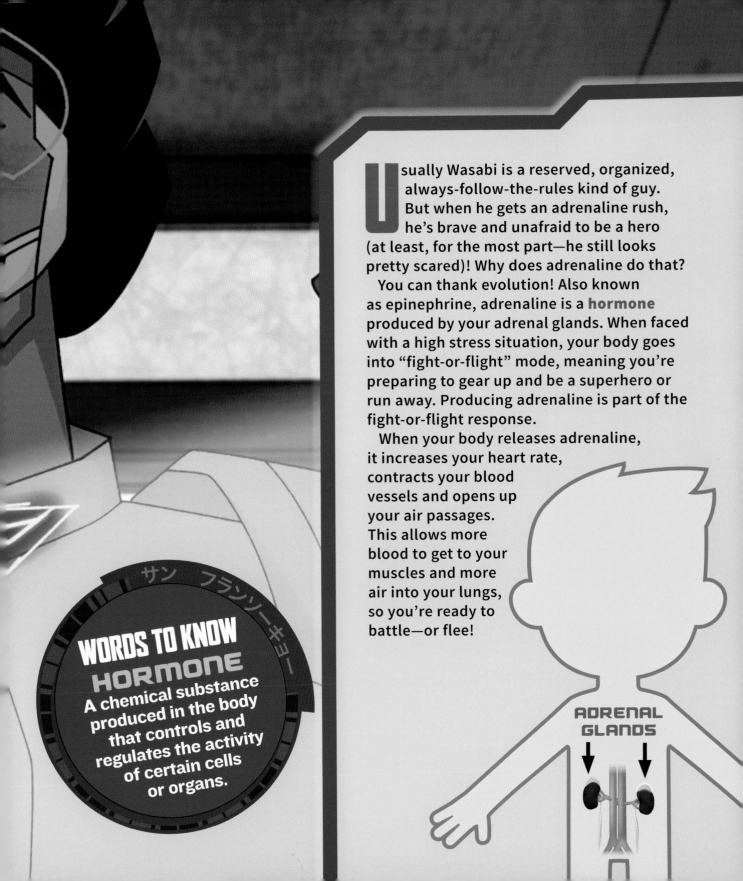

Usually Wasabi is a reserved, organized, always-follow-the-rules kind of guy. But when he gets an adrenaline rush, he's brave and unafraid to be a hero (at least, for the most part—he still looks pretty scared)! Why does adrenaline do that?

You can thank evolution! Also known as epinephrine, adrenaline is a **hormone** produced by your adrenal glands. When faced with a high stress situation, your body goes into "fight-or-flight" mode, meaning you're preparing to gear up and be a superhero or run away. Producing adrenaline is part of the fight-or-flight response.

When your body releases adrenaline, it increases your heart rate, contracts your blood vessels and opens up your air passages. This allows more blood to get to your muscles and more air into your lungs, so you're ready to battle—or flee!

ADRENAL
GLANDS

WORDS TO KNOW
HORMONE
A chemical substance produced in the body that controls and regulates the activity of certain cells or organs.

サン　フランシスキョー

WORDS TO KNOW

MOTOR PROCESSES
Activity in the muscles of the body that you can control, also known as "voluntary" activity.

WHY DO PEOPLE SAY "OW" WHEN THEY FEEL PAIN?

HELLO. I AM BAYMAX. I WAS ALERTED TO THE NEED FOR MEDICAL ATTENTION WHEN YOU SAID, "OW."

Fred, Wasabi and Honey Lemon each get knocked out by Mr. Sparkles's Maximum Insane Obstacle Challenge in their attempt to save Mochi. Getting hit with stuff can be painful—just ask Wasabi what it was like when he got hit by a giant piece of broccoli!

According to research from the National University of Singapore, saying "ow" actually helps you tolerate pain. The researchers hypothesize that it has something to do with **motor processes.** They think that because your body has to focus on making the noise, it may disrupt the pain messages being sent to your brain.

The researchers tested their hypothesis by having 56 volunteers put their hands in painfully cold water. Each person was asked to either say "ow," listen to a recording of someone saying "ow," to stay quiet and still or to press a button. Volunteers who were asked to say "ow" or to press a button reported that it helped them tolerate the pain, but those who did nothing or just listened to someone saying "ow" did not.

WHY DO PEOPLE CRY?

When Hiro needs to get close enough to Professor Granville to copy her key card credentials, he decides to fake a few tears. Hugging Professor Granville gives just enough time for the transfer to work!

There are three types of tears: basal, reflex and psychic. Basal tears keep the cornea lubricated so the eye doesn't dry out. Reflex tears flush any irritants, like onion vapors, out of the eye. Psychic tears are the ones that appear when you are "crying," as they happen in response to emotions and physical pain. Psychic tears also contain something called leucine enkephalin, which is a natural painkiller.

Tears are made in the lacrimal gland, which is located in between the eyeball and the eyelid. Some tears will drain through the nose via the tear sac (that's why people often get a runny nose when they cry), but the rest will overflow over the lower eyelids.

Each part of your eye has a different purpose:

SCLERA
Also known as the white of the eye, this is the protective layer that makes up more than 80 percent of the eye's surface area.

PUPIL
Allows light to enter.

LACRIMAL GLAND

TEAR SAC

IRIS
The colored part of your eye, it changes the size of your pupils to allow more or less light in. Your pupils appear bigger when it's dark because your iris has retracted to allow more light into your eye.

WHY DO HUGS MAKE PEOPLE FEEL BETTER?

WOULD YOU LIKE A HUG?

Baymax knows the power of a good hug. When you hug someone, your body releases a hormone called oxytocin. Oxytocin makes people feel good! What's more, hugs activate pressure receptors in your skin. These pressure receptors, called Pacinian corpuscles, send signals to the vagus nerve in your brain, which lowers your blood pressure and helps you calm down.

WHERE DOES OXYTOCIN COME FROM?

Oxytocin comes from the hypothalamus region of the brain. It's then released by the pituitary gland into the bloodstream.

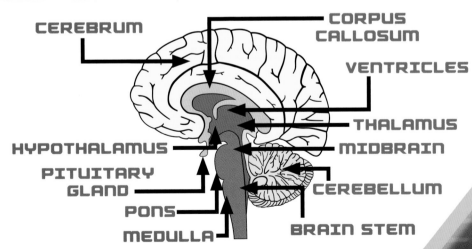

CEREBRUM

CORPUS CALLOSUM

VENTRICLES

THALAMUS

HYPOTHALAMUS

MIDBRAIN

PITUITARY GLAND

CEREBELLUM

PONS

BRAIN STEM

MEDULLA

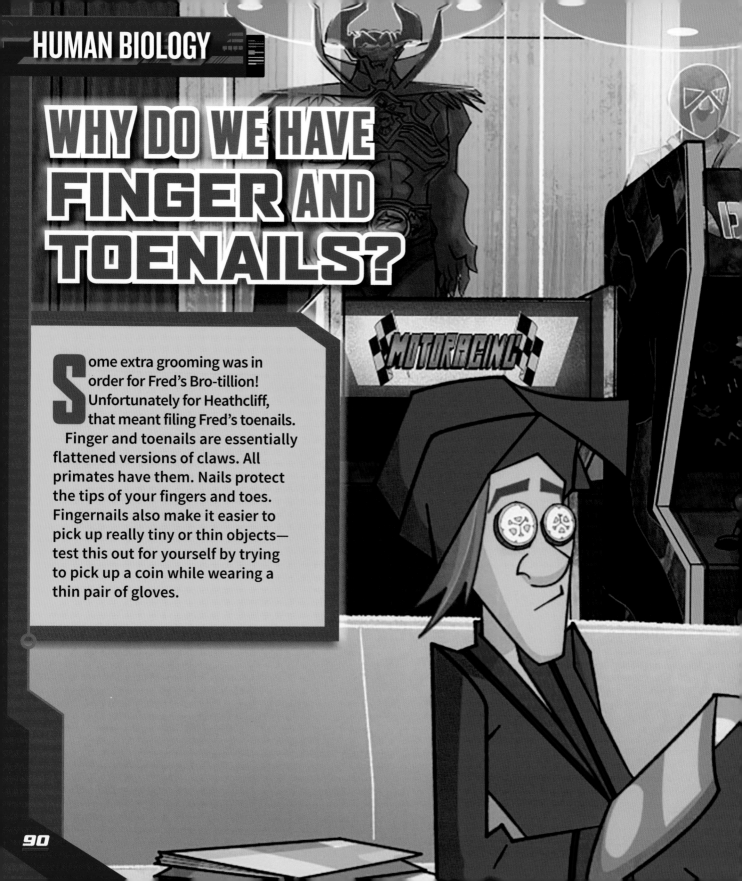

WHY DO WE HAVE FINGER AND TOENAILS?

Some extra grooming was in order for Fred's Bro-tillion! Unfortunately for Heathcliff, that meant filing Fred's toenails. Finger and toenails are essentially flattened versions of claws. All primates have them. Nails protect the tips of your fingers and toes. Fingernails also make it easier to pick up really tiny or thin objects— test this out for yourself by trying to pick up a coin while wearing a thin pair of gloves.

CRITICAL THINKING

Toenails are two to three times thicker than fingernails, but they grow more slowly. Scientists don't know for sure why that is, but they have some hypotheses. One popular theory is that nail growth is linked to blood flow, while other scientists think the more you use your fingers, the faster the nails grow. What sorts of experiments would you use to try to test these theories?

WHY DO SCIENTISTS WEAR BIOHAZARD SUITS?

UM, SHOULD I BE WEARING A BIOHAZARD SUIT?

Karmi wears a biohazard suit while observing her mutated viruses. It's a good precaution to take when working with dangerous organisms!

Scientists wear biohazard suits when conducting experiments like these, or when working with dangerous chemicals or gases. Also known as hazmat suits, this protective clothing keeps a person from coming in contact with any kind of hazardous material.

WHY DO SICK PEOPLE SNEEZE?

When Hiro has a cold, one of the first signs is his sneezing! That's because your body sneezes whenever an irritant, like pet dander or a cold virus, gets past your nose hairs. The sneeze is your body's attempt to keep out the irritant. A cold virus, for example, tickles the nerve endings in the lining of your nose, which sends a signal to your brain. Your brain responds by shutting your eyes and contracting the muscles in your throat, causing a sneeze that clears the bacteria from your nose at an impressive 30–40 mph.

A SNEEZE IS A SEMI-AUTONOMOUS CONVULSION OF AIR.

WHY DO PEOPLE NEED SLEEP?

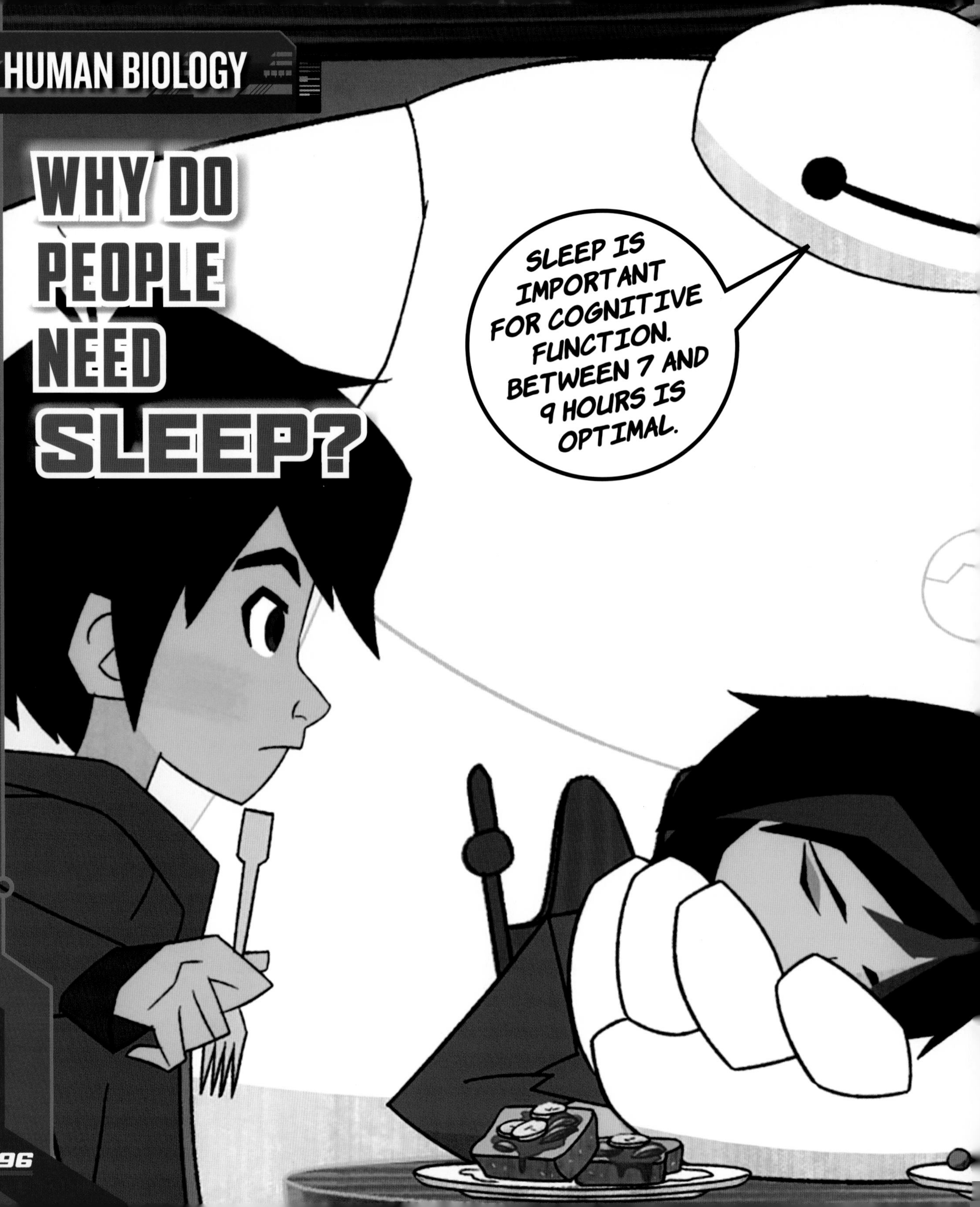

After Honey Lemon moves in with Go Go, her snoring keeps Go Go from getting a decent night's sleep!

Though sleep is something we're all very familiar with, scientists still don't know exactly why we need it. The obvious answer is that animals need sleep in order to properly rest—though it's unclear why we need to rest in the first place. But we do know our bodies are doing a lot of important work while they're asleep.

For example, while you're sleeping, your brain is transferring short-term memories into long-term memories. Your body also does a lot of healing while you're asleep: muscles grow and tissues are repaired during long periods of rest.

CRITICAL THINKING

Scientists have noticed that many mammals living in groups only sleep when at least one member of the group is awake. Why do you think this occurs? Can you think of a connection between this behavior and people who are "night owls"?

WHY IS IT WEIRD TO BE WOKEN UP ABRUPTLY?

Waking up doesn't have to be shocking, but when Fred shines the HALP sign into Hiro's room, it startles him from a deep sleep.

You've probably noticed that when you wake up naturally, you're usually not groggy and you feel refreshed. But sometimes being woken up while you're sleeping can be jarring and disorienting—that means you were in stage 3 or 4 sleep, when your brain waves were moving very slowly.

ALL SLEEP IS NOT THE SAME.
In fact, people go through different stages of sleep, known as the sleep cycle.

STAGE 1 Light sleep, during which you drift in and out of consciousness and can be woken easily. The eyes move slowly and sudden muscle contractions may happen.

STAGE 2 Eye movement stops, brain waves become slower and the body temperature drops as the body prepares for deep sleep.

STAGE 3 This is deep sleep. Extremely slow brain waves occur, along with occasional bursts of smaller, faster brain waves.

STAGE 4 This is very deep sleep. People who are woken during stage 4 sleep feel disoriented for a few minutes.

REM SLEEP REM stands for rapid eye movement. During REM sleep, brain waves are similar to being awake. The eyes move around a lot, and intense dreaming occurs.

A full sleep cycle lasts between 90 and 120 minutes, with people commonly progressing from stages 1 through 4, then back to stages 3, 2 and then 1. This is followed by a period of REM sleep, and then the cycle begins again.

WHY DO SOME PEOPLE TALK IN THEIR SLEEP?

Even though Honey Lemon is trying her best to keep her status as an art student a secret, Go Go already knows—Honey Lemon told her in her sleep!

Also known as somniloquy, scientists aren't entirely sure why some people talk in their sleep (though stress can be a trigger, so that might explain why Honey Lemon was doing it). It can happen during any stage of sleep, and most people have no idea they're doing it until someone tells them. It's a bit of a mystery, just like other parasomnias, such as sleepwalking and nocturnal sleep-related eating disorder (NSRED), a condition that causes people to eat while they're asleep.

WORDS TO KNOW

PARASOMNIA

Parasomnias are abnormal things that happen while a person sleeps.

WHY DO PEOPLE DROOL IN THEIR SLEEP?

WORDS TO KNOW

SALIVARY GLAND

The glands that produce saliva, salivary glands are located on the inside of each cheek, and under the jaw at the front of the mouth and at the bottom of the mouth.

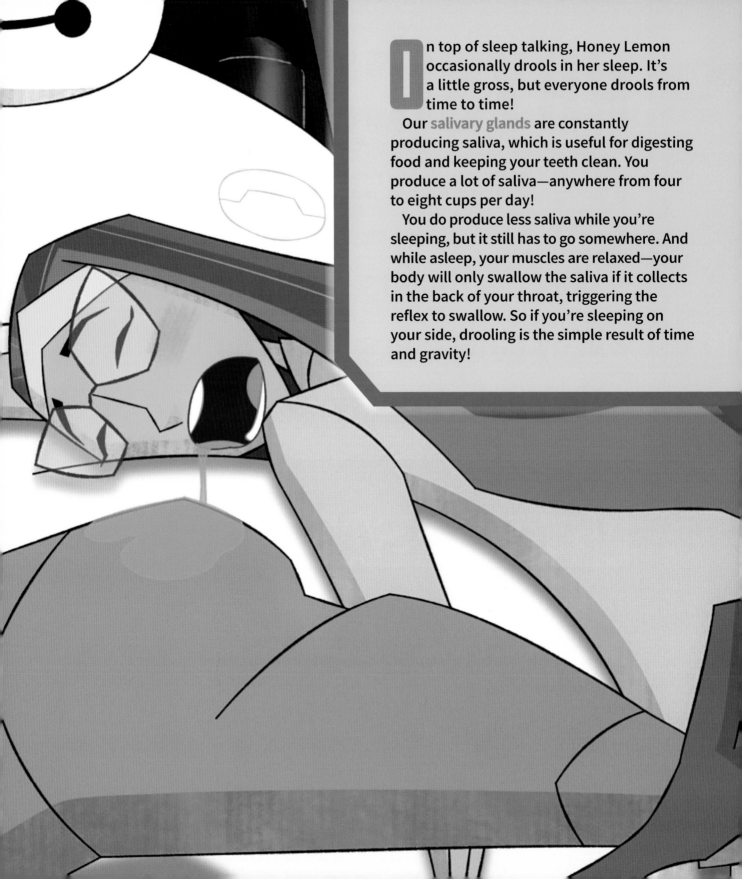

On top of sleep talking, Honey Lemon occasionally drools in her sleep. It's a little gross, but everyone drools from time to time!

Our **salivary glands** are constantly producing saliva, which is useful for digesting food and keeping your teeth clean. You produce a lot of saliva—anywhere from four to eight cups per day!

You do produce less saliva while you're sleeping, but it still has to go somewhere. And while asleep, your muscles are relaxed—your body will only swallow the saliva if it collects in the back of your throat, triggering the reflex to swallow. So if you're sleeping on your side, drooling is the simple result of time and gravity!

PHYSICS

Physics is the scientific study of matter and energy and all the different interactions between the two.

When thinking about physics, you might have questions like...

- **Why do objects retain heat?**
- **Why can lasers burn things?**
- **How does gravity work?**

MEET WASABI

Though he's usually a very careful person who abides by the rules, Wasabi took a risk when his friends needed him the most and became part of Big Hero 6. Incredibly intelligent (and just a little tightly wound), Wasabi is highly organized and all about precision, which makes him the ideal physicist. Combined with his karate skills and laser knowledge, he's also pretty great at taking down villains!

WHAT IS PLASMA?

Wasabi's plasma blades are a truly incredible piece of tech! Plasma is the fourth state of matter (the other three are solids, liquids and gases). Plasma is made when energy is added to a gas, causing its atoms and molecules to separate into negatively charged electrons and positively charged ions. This process is called ionization. Plasma is naturally made by lightning, though scientists have figured out how to create it artificially as well.

Plasma behaves differently than other states of matter. It reacts strongly to electric and magnetic fields, and it's a great conductor of electricity—even better than copper!

CRITICAL THINKING

Scientists are experimenting with plasma to create something called fusion, a new kind of nuclear power that would be safer and create less radioactive waste than the current process. Why do you think it's important to come up with new kinds of power sources?

WORDS TO KNOW

KINETIC ENERGY

Energy that comes from motion.

WHY DO OBJECTS RETAIN HEAT?

Aunt Cass uses her kitten-shaped oven mitts when carrying a plate that's hot. But why doesn't the plate immediately cool off? Because that heat is a form of kinetic energy.

Heat is a form of energy found in almost everything, from a fire to an ice cube. Heat energy flows from substance to substance, causing their molecules to move and bump around. An object with very low heat energy will have very still molecules, causing it to slow down and eventually freeze. Objects with higher heat energy will get hotter and less dense until they change states, becoming a liquid and eventually a gas.

Objects remain hot after being exposed to a heat source because the molecules are still bouncing around from the heat energy they received.

WHY DOES ICE MELT?

The ice sculpture of Fred for his Bro-tillion looks pretty awesome, but unless they get it in a freezer, it will be gone pretty soon! Water is a perfect example of a substance that transforms between various states of matter. Ice is water's "solid state," meaning that all of its molecules are locked in a rigid, compact form. Solids have a fixed shape, which makes them easy to pick up or hold. However, heating up a solid will cause the molecules to become charged with heat energy, causing them to move around and break their formation. This causes an object to transform into liquid, a state of matter where molecules touch but aren't packed together. Ice freezes at 32 degrees Fahrenheit, if it's in a place warmer than that, it will melt.

WHY CAN'T ANY OBJECT GO FASTER THAN THE SPEED OF LIGHT?

When Fred turns on the HALP signal he made for Big Hero 6, it seems to appear in the sky instantaneously. That's because the speed of light is so incredibly fast—it's 186,282 miles per second!

Nothing solid can travel this fast because having mass increases the amount of energy needed to accelerate. Think of it this way: It takes more energy to push a heavy cart than a light cart, and even more energy to push a heavy cart at a fast speed. Imagine having to move anything with mass as fast as the speed of light—as far as scientists know, it's impossible. There isn't enough energy in the entire universe to accelerate a single electron to the speed of light!

WHY DOES LAVA GLOW?

After Baron Von Steamer kidnaps Wasabi, confusing him for Fred, he almost drops him into a giant pit of glowing lava! Lava, molten rock from the Earth's mantle, shines with a red hot glow. And boy is it hot, reaching temperatures of 2,200 degrees Fahrenheit! In fact, the heat is the reason lava glows. Like everything else, lava is made up of atoms, and the enormous amount of heat energy from its extreme temperature causes those atoms' electrons to boost to a higher orbit than normal. In order for the electron to return to its regular orbit, it must release the excess energy, which it does in the form of light. This cycle of the electrons getting excited and then releasing that heat energy by glowing continues for as long as the lava stays that hot!

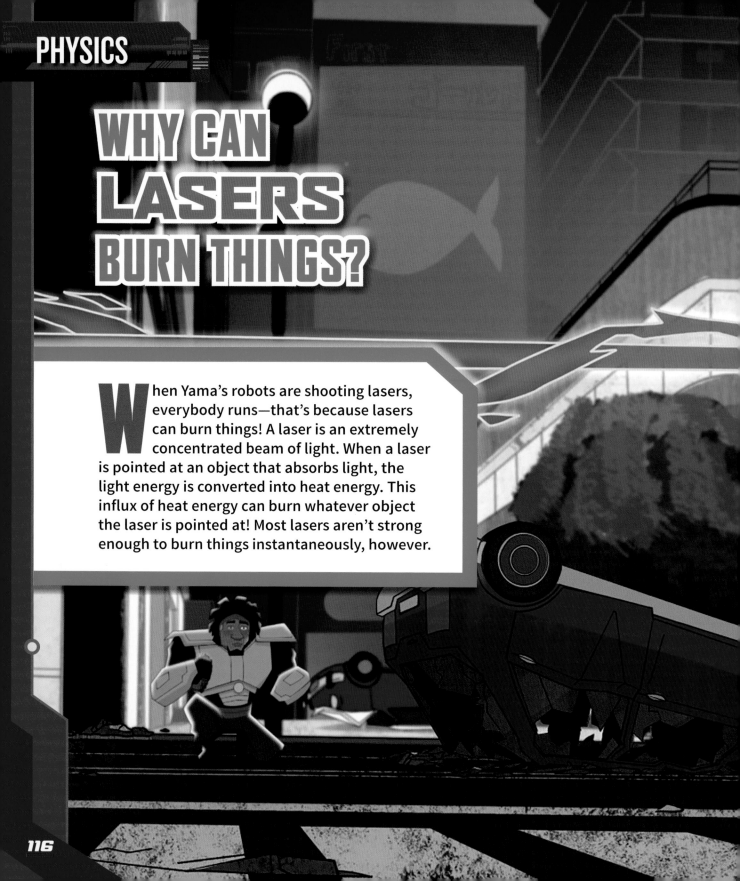

WHY CAN LASERS BURN THINGS?

When Yama's robots are shooting lasers, everybody runs—that's because lasers can burn things! A laser is an extremely concentrated beam of light. When a laser is pointed at an object that absorbs light, the light energy is converted into heat energy. This influx of heat energy can burn whatever object the laser is pointed at! Most lasers aren't strong enough to burn things instantaneously, however.

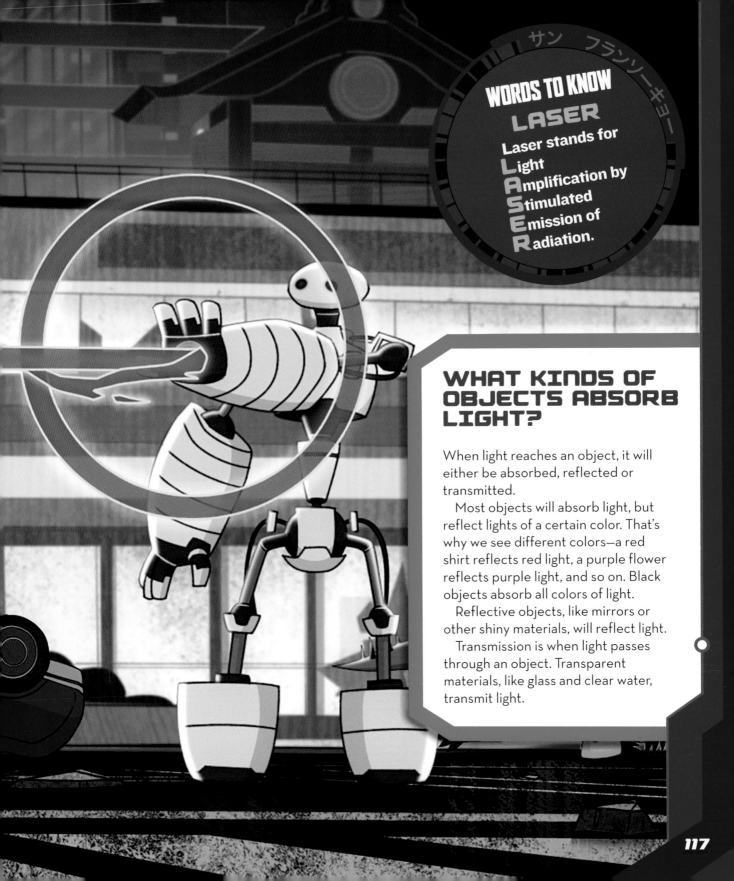

WORDS TO KNOW
LASER
Laser stands for
Light
Amplification by
Stimulated
Emission of
Radiation.

WHAT KINDS OF OBJECTS ABSORB LIGHT?

When light reaches an object, it will either be absorbed, reflected or transmitted.

Most objects will absorb light, but reflect lights of a certain color. That's why we see different colors—a red shirt reflects red light, a purple flower reflects purple light, and so on. Black objects absorb all colors of light.

Reflective objects, like mirrors or other shiny materials, will reflect light.

Transmission is when light passes through an object. Transparent materials, like glass and clear water, transmit light.

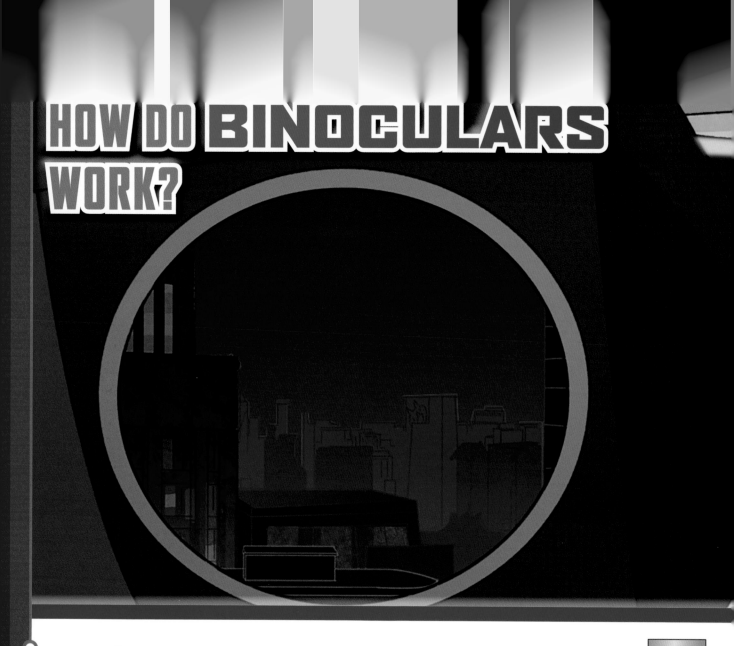

HOW DO BINOCULARS WORK?

Because he doesn't have super sight (though he probably wishes he did), Fred needs to use binoculars when scanning San Fransokyo for danger.

Binoculars are essentially two convex telescopes that are attached to each other. A convex telescope uses a technique called **refraction** in order to make objects appear closer to you. Refracting telescopes use two lenses, a small one that you look through and a larger one at the opposite end. The larger lens catches the image that you're looking at. It's then reflected off of two more lenses within the binoculars. Finally, the smaller lens works like a magnifying glass that enlarges the image.

サン　フランシスキョー

WORDS TO KNOW

REFRACTION

Refraction is the
bending of light as it
passes through a
substance.

WHY DO MAGNETS REPEL ONE ANOTHER?

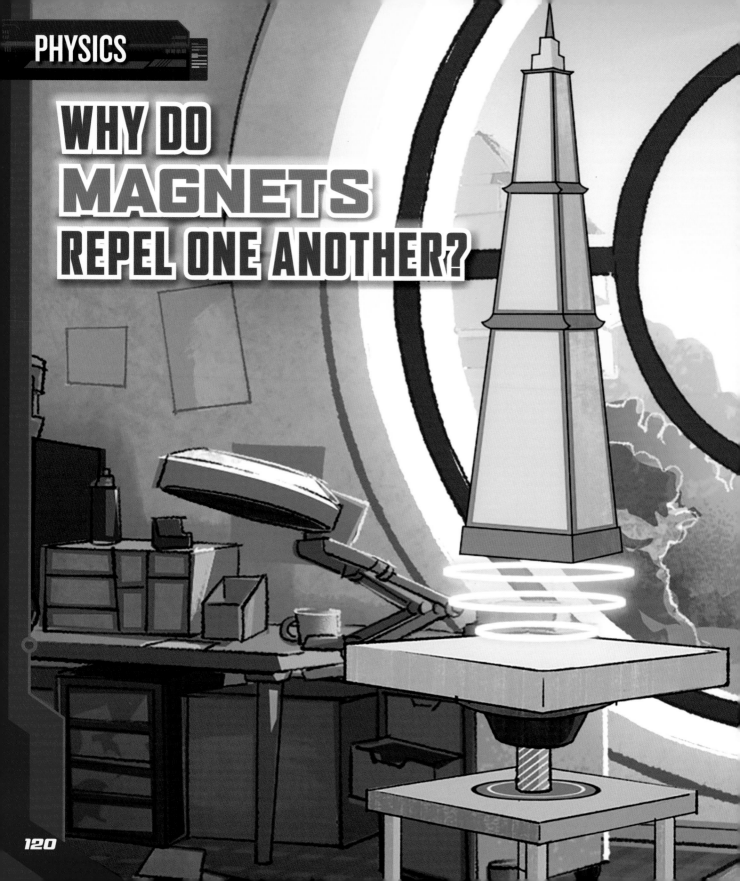

Hiro had a hard time coming up with an original idea for his homework assignment. Maglev fields, foam cushions and airbags have all been done by his friends! Go Go's idea, of course, had been to use magnetic levitation.

Magnets have fields of electricity coursing through them. These fields of electricity create poles at either end of the magnet. Electricity enters the magnet at the south pole and exits it at the north pole. When you try to put a north pole from one magnet up against the north pole from the other magnet, the exiting electricity will force them apart. Similarly, the electricity entering the south pole keeps two south poles from being pressed together. But if a north pole meets a south pole, the electricity flows from one into the other, making them attract!

YEP, THAT'S WHAT I DID WHEN I WAS A FRESHMAN.

HOW DOES GRAVITY WORK?

Big Hero 6 attempts to get back the gravity disruptor Momakase stole, but it accidentally goes off while they're fighting! Without warning, everything in the Food Fight arena begins to float, and everyone finds out what it would be like to live in a world without gravity.

Every object that has mass exerts a gravitational pull on every other mass in the universe. The more mass an object has, the stronger its gravitational pull. On Earth, the Earth itself is what has the most mass, so everything is pulled toward it. The moon has considerably less mass, which is why astronauts don't feel as much of a gravitational pull when they're on the moon. In our whole solar system, though, the sun has the most mass—that's why all the planets orbit it.

WHY DOESN'T THE EARTH GET PULLED INTO THE SUN?

The Earth is always falling toward the sun, but because the Earth is also moving sideways, it orbits the sun rather than colliding with it. Imagine swinging a ball on a string: It's constantly being pulled toward your hand, but the sideways movement causes it to move in a circle instead of falling directly into your hand.

CRITICAL THINKING
All objects are equally affected by gravity, regardless of their size. You can test this out yourself: Drop a baseball and a penny from the same height at the same time, and they'll both hit the ground simultaneously! You'll notice that things like feathers and inflated balloons don't fall as quickly, though—why do you think that is?

WHAT ARE NEWTON'S THREE LAWS OF MOTION?

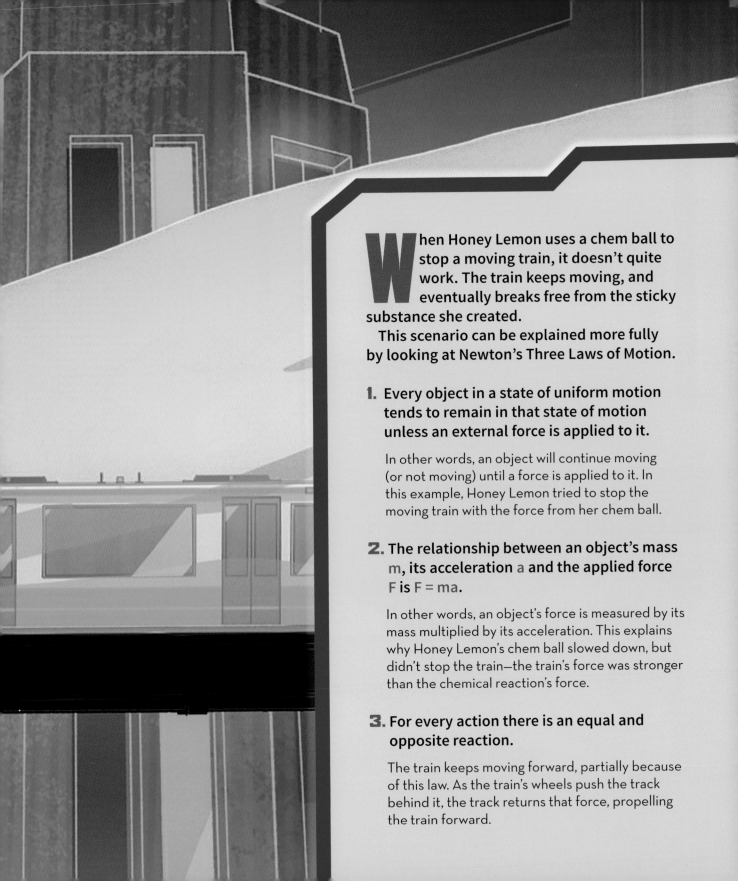

When Honey Lemon uses a chem ball to stop a moving train, it doesn't quite work. The train keeps moving, and eventually breaks free from the sticky substance she created.

This scenario can be explained more fully by looking at Newton's Three Laws of Motion.

1. **Every object in a state of uniform motion tends to remain in that state of motion unless an external force is applied to it.**

   In other words, an object will continue moving (or not moving) until a force is applied to it. In this example, Honey Lemon tried to stop the moving train with the force from her chem ball.

2. **The relationship between an object's mass m, its acceleration a and the applied force F is $F = ma$.**

   In other words, an object's force is measured by its mass multiplied by its acceleration. This explains why Honey Lemon's chem ball slowed down, but didn't stop the train—the train's force was stronger than the chemical reaction's force.

3. **For every action there is an equal and opposite reaction.**

   The train keeps moving forward, partially because of this law. As the train's wheels push the track behind it, the track returns that force, propelling the train forward.

WHY IS SPEED DIFFERENT FROM VELOCITY?

Whenever Go Go zooms by on her maglev discs, she's not just picking up speed—she also has velocity!

Speed is a **scalar quantity** and velocity is a **vector quantity**. In other words, speed is a measure of how fast something is moving, and velocity is the rate of speed in a given direction. So Go Go's speed might be 50 mph, but her velocity would be 50 mph east (or whichever direction she's headed in).

WORDS TO KNOW

SCALAR QUANTITY
A measurement that is only defined by a number, like volume or speed.

VECTOR QUANTITY
A measure that includes a number and a direction, like velocity.

CRITICAL THINKING
Why is it important for scientists to differentiate between speed and velocity? Knowing a velocity is important if you need to determine exactly where something is going. Just imagine planning a space mission and knowing how fast your rocket is going, but not knowing its direction!

WHY DO BOATS FLOAT?

海 船

Fred may have crashed his boat into a building, but at least it didn't sink. That's because boats are buoyant! When a boat's weight pushes it down into the water, the water pushes back up, keeping it above the waves. This happens because the boat is less dense than the amount of water it is displacing. To make sure a boat sails safely and does not sink, engineers determine the maximum amount of weight that is allowed, to make sure the density of the boat does not surpass the density of the water. The shape of a boat also helps it float. Extremely large boats often have flat bottoms because it gives the water more space to push up against.

WORDS TO KNOW
DENSITY
Density is a measurement of mass divided by volume, or how much mass is compressed into a certain amount of space. The more dense something is, the more heavy it is by volume. A rock is very dense, which is why it sinks in water. A piece of wood is less dense than water, so it floats.

WHY ARE MOTORCYCLES SO LOUD?

Honey Lemon gives Felony Carl's motorcycle a makeover, turning it pink and sparkly. This doesn't change how loud it is, though!

Sound is a vibration that travels through matter, like a solid, liquid or gas. Sound travels most easily through gases, which are less dense than liquids or solids. Some owners want their motorcycles to be extra loud, so they remove the muffler, a piece of equipment designed to muffle the sound of the engine. Without the solid muffler, the sound can travel through the air more easily!

HOW DO WE MEASURE THE VOLUME OF SOUND?

Sound is measured in units called decibels. The louder a sound is, the more decibels it has.

For example

Pin dropping 10 decibels
Normal conversation 60 decibels
Alarm clock 80 decibels
Motorcycle engine 100 decibels
Jet engine 140 decibels
Rocket launch 180 decibels

WHY DO ONLY SOME MATERIALS CONDUCT ELECTRICITY?

Mom and daughter duo Barb and Juniper are High Voltage, villains who use electric whips to steal money (and also put on pretty impressive dance shows). Honey Lemon realizes she can slow these villains down with some materials their electricity won't work on.

The only solid materials that conduct electricity are metals and graphite. This has to do with their atomic structure. Metal atoms have outer valence electrons which are free to move about. It's these electrons and their ability to move around that lets them conduct electricity. Water can also be a good conductor of electricity, as long as it's not distilled! Pure water does not conduct electricity, but natural "plain" water often has minerals dissolved in it, like iron and magnesium. These charged minerals allow electricity to flow through the liquid.

RUBBER INSULATES ELECTRICITY!

CRITICAL THINKING
When Honey Lemon surrounds
High Voltage with rubber, it prevents
them from using their electric tech.
Why do you think that is?

WHY DO POWER SURGES HAPPEN?

Baymax gets hit with an electrical surge while battling High Voltage, causing him to short circuit. Power surges, also called voltage spikes, happen when a flow of electricity is interrupted and then started again, or when an outside source (like Juniper's electric whip) sends a surge of electricity into the power system. Power surges can affect microprocessors and their ability to function properly.

POWER POWER POWER SURGE!

WORDS TO KNOW
VOLTAGE
Voltage is the pressure that pushes an electical current through a conducting loop.

WHY DOES STATIC SHOCK OCCUR?

Mochi's fur stands on its end after Baymax has been petting him! This is because of static electricity.

Static electricity often causes static cling, and the occasional static shock. When two different materials (like Baymax's exterior and Mochi's fur) rub against each other, one surface will pick up some electrons from the other surface. At this point the surfaces have different charges, one positive and one negative. Opposite charges attract, causing the materials to cling together. This also explains static shock: If you happen to have an excess of electrons on your body, you'll feel a small zap when they transfer to a new material, like a doorknob or your friend's finger!

NATURE

Studying nature is another way of studying biology and earth science! When you examine nature, you might have questions like…

- **How do caterpillars become butterflies?**

- **Why do flowers need sunlight?**

- **Why does wind blow?**

MEET FRED!

Fred is the unofficial school mascot for the San Fransokyo Institute of Technology. He's not an expert in science, though he is curious about the world around him and is constantly amazed by the incredible things his friends create. Fred is also an important member of Big Hero 6—his knowledge of comic books and ability to think outside the box often come in handy!

WHY DOES FISH SMELL?

Aunt Cass does a good job of grossing out everyone else on the train when her arms are full of butterfish! Fish smells worse than other kinds of meat because of a certain chemical in fish tissue called trimethylamine (try-ma-thigh-la-mean) oxide. When that chemical starts to break down, it becomes two new chemicals that are derivatives of ammonia—and ammonia smells very, very bad. Adding something acidic helps those two new chemicals break down, so hopefully Aunt Cass cooks those butterfish with some lemon or vinegar.

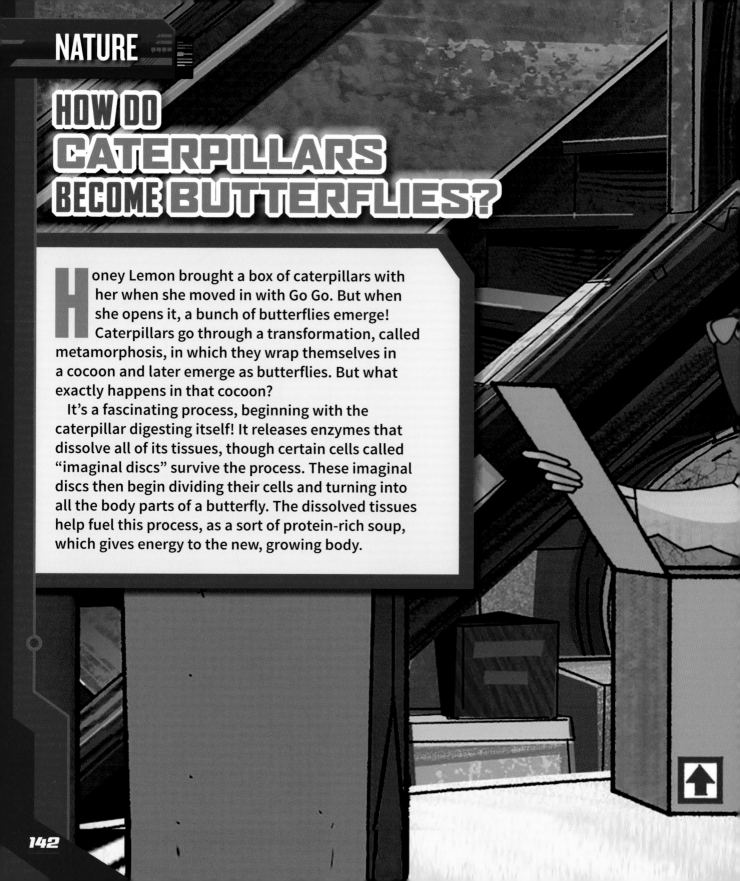

HOW DO CATERPILLARS BECOME BUTTERFLIES?

Honey Lemon brought a box of caterpillars with her when she moved in with Go Go. But when she opens it, a bunch of butterflies emerge! Caterpillars go through a transformation, called metamorphosis, in which they wrap themselves in a cocoon and later emerge as butterflies. But what exactly happens in that cocoon?

It's a fascinating process, beginning with the caterpillar digesting itself! It releases enzymes that dissolve all of its tissues, though certain cells called "imaginal discs" survive the process. These imaginal discs then begin dividing their cells and turning into all the body parts of a butterfly. The dissolved tissues help fuel this process, as a sort of protein-rich soup, which gives energy to the new, growing body.

CATERPILLARS

WHY DO FLOWERS GIVE OFF SCENTS?

Honey Lemon loves the smell of fresh flowers! She brought her own when moving in with Go Go.

Some flowers smell good, hoping to attract bees and insects which will help them pollinate. Other plants emit smells to deter predators from eating them!

Plants have other defense mechanisms, too. Some are poisonous. And many plants, like roses, succulents and wild raspberry bushes, have thorns and prickles (which are just smaller thorns) to defend themselves from animals or insects that attempt to eat them.

CRITICAL THINKING
Some plants produce fruits
that smell and taste good.
Why would a plant want
its fruit to be eaten?
Think about the seeds.

WHY DO CATS SLEEP SO MUCH?

More often than not, Mochi can be found dozing away somewhere in Aunt Cass's house! This isn't surprising, as most cats sleep for around 15 hours a day.

Cats are natural predators and sleep so much in order to build up energy. They are not fully domesticated, which means they're naturally prepared to use a lot of energy to hunt their own food. Cats are also crepuscular creatures, which means they're most active at dusk and dawn—that's why they sleep so much during the day.

WHY DO CATS HAVE WHISKERS?

A cat's whiskers, or vibrissae, are actually very useful tools. When a cat's whiskers brush against something, it immediately receives information on the size, texture and location of the object, helping the cat navigate in the dark. A cat's whiskers also alert it of changes in air currents, which can help them sense danger.

WHY DO OCTOPUSES HAVE SUCKERS ON THEIR ARMS?

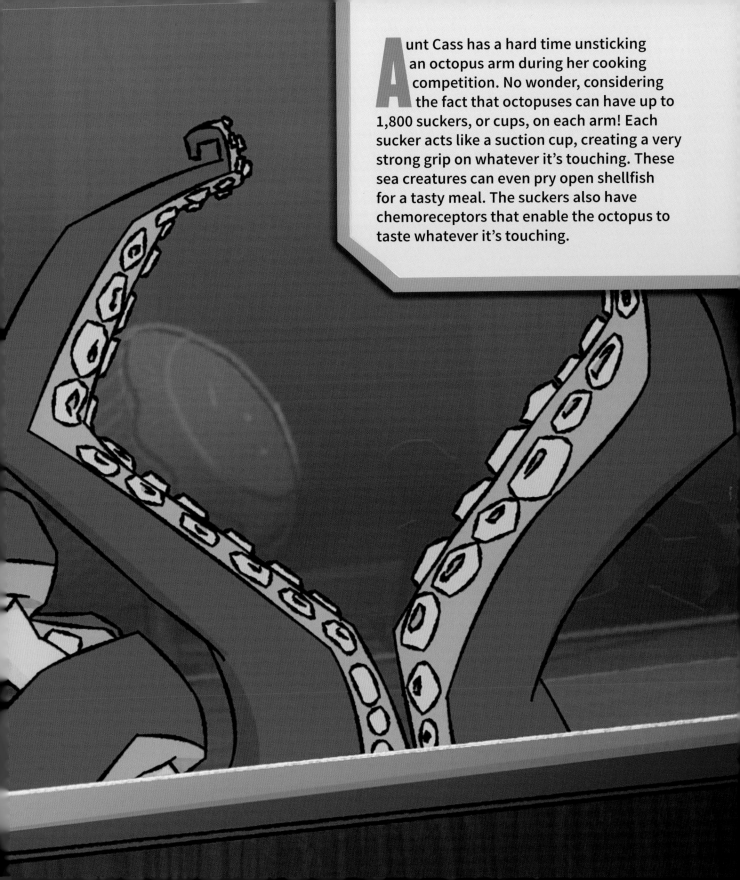

Aunt Cass has a hard time unsticking an octopus arm during her cooking competition. No wonder, considering the fact that octopuses can have up to 1,800 suckers, or cups, on each arm! Each sucker acts like a suction cup, creating a very strong grip on whatever it's touching. These sea creatures can even pry open shellfish for a tasty meal. The suckers also have chemoreceptors that enable the octopus to taste whatever it's touching.

WHY ARE THEY CALLED DUNG BEETLES?

During a trip out of the city, Hiro gets very up close and personal with nature—he even gets a dung beetle on his face!

Dung beetles earned their name by hanging around a lot of poop. The beetles roll manure into balls, bring the balls underground, burrow inside and then feed on them. (Pretty gross!) Later, female beetles will deposit their eggs into dung balls. Once the eggs hatch, the beetle larvae will also feed on the balls.

CRITICAL THINKING

The dung beetle's way of life is pretty off-putting to humans, but they're great for the environment! In parts of Texas, dung beetles bury about 80 percent of cow dung. What do you think it would be like if we didn't have dung beetles?

WHY DO LIGHTNING BUGS GLOW?

Because electronics don't work in Muirahara Woods, Ned uses lightning bugs to fill his lamp when it's dark out.

Lightning bugs, also called fireflies, have their special ability because they are bioluminescent. Their abdomens contain a chemical compound called luciferin. As air enters the abdomen, it reacts with the luciferin, making the firefly light up. The fireflies can control when air enters their abdomens, enabling them to create specific patterns. Scientists think fireflies light up to look for partners, or to trick other species of firefly into coming close and becoming a meal!

サン　フランシキョー

WORDS TO KNOW
BIOLUMINESCENCE
The creation and release of light by a living organism. Lightning bugs are the most famous example, but lots of marine creatures are also bioluminescent, like certain types of jellyfish, worms, seastars, crustaceans and even sharks!

WHY DO FLOWERS NEED SUNLIGHT?

Baymax does some odd things in Muirahara Woods, like petting flowers! Flowers don't enjoy being petted, but they do enjoy getting plenty of sunlight.

Without light, plants wouldn't exist—and that would completely upend our ecosystem. Plants need light, water and carbon dioxide to create food. They use chlorophyll (a green pigment that absorbs light) to absorb energy from the sun; collect water and minerals through their roots; and carbon dioxide from the air, which passes through pores in their leaves. This process is called photosynthesis.

ENERGY from sunlight

Plant releases **OXYGEN**

Plant uses carbon dioxide and hydrogen to make **GLUCOSE**

CARBON DIOXIDE is absorbed from the air

WATER AND MINERALS Absorbed from the soil through the roots.

Photosynthesis is broken down like this:

1. Plants use the sunlight's energy to split water molecules into hydrogen and oxygen.

2. The hydrogen they produce and carbon dioxide they take in are used to form glucose, which is their source of food.

3. Plants release oxygen, a byproduct of photosynthesis. This is one of the many reasons plants are so important to the earth—we need oxygen to breathe! If plants had no light, we wouldn't have the oxygen we need to survive.

WHY DO HONEY BEES MAKE HIVES?

Baymax meets some honey bees while he is lost in the Muirhara Woods! Honey bees make hives in order to store all their honey. They build them by chewing wax until it becomes pliable, and then use the soft wax to create honeycombs. Even the honeycomb shape is purposeful: the six-sided tubes require less wax to make and can hold more honey than other shapes. When a lot of worker honey bees are together in the hive, their body heat keeps it at a toasty 85–95 degrees Fahrenheit, the perfect temperature for maintaining the waxy texture.

WHY DO BEE STINGS HURT?

When a bee stings you, it injects a tiny bit of venom in your body, which can hurt a lot! But with some chemistry knowledge, you can treat the sting. Bee stings are acidic, which means they can be neutralized with a substance that is a base. Baking soda is a good choice!

WHY ARE SOME FROGS BRIGHTLY COLORED?

While in the children's science museum, Baymax meets some brightly colored frogs. They're very attention-grabbing, and that's no accident.

Some frogs are brightly colored in order to warn predators that they are poisonous. Interestingly, of the predators that eat frogs, birds are the only ones that see all the different colors of poisonous frogs. That suggests frogs evolved their bright colors because at one point, birds were their biggest threat.

CRITICAL THINKING
Birds can see all the different colors of frogs, but they aren't very good at detecting how bright a color is. Still, some frogs are dull-colored, while others are especially bright. What reasons can you come up with that would explain this?

WHY DO RIVERS HAVE CURRENTS?

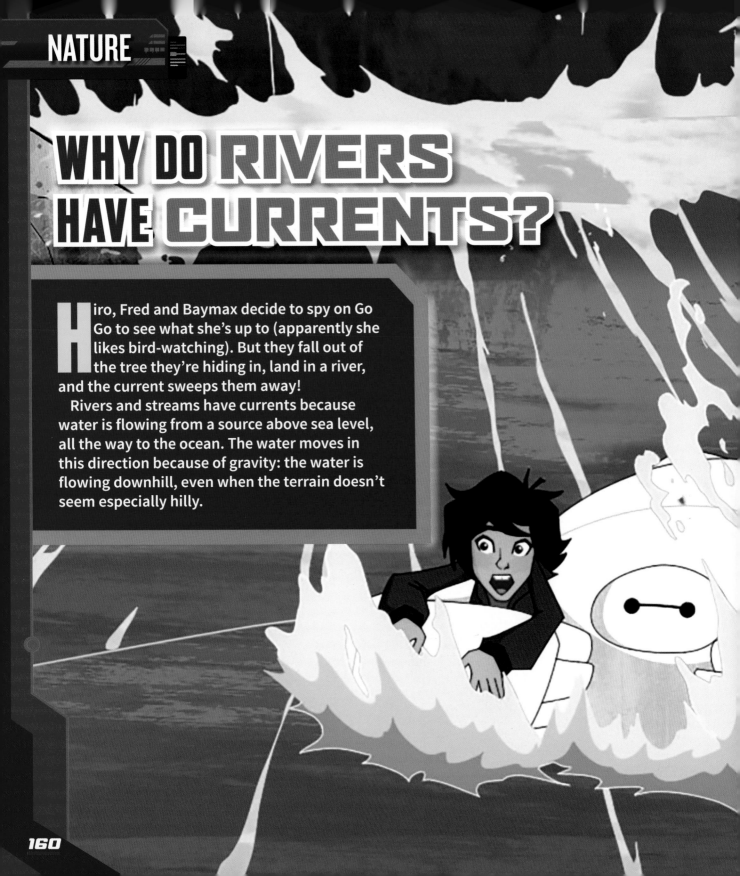

Hiro, Fred and Baymax decide to spy on Go Go to see what she's up to (apparently she likes bird-watching). But they fall out of the tree they're hiding in, land in a river, and the current sweeps them away!

Rivers and streams have currents because water is flowing from a source above sea level, all the way to the ocean. The water moves in this direction because of gravity: the water is flowing downhill, even when the terrain doesn't seem especially hilly.

HOW DO WE TURN WATER CURRENTS INTO USABLE ENERGY?

Engineers have invented hydroelectric plants that turn water currents into electricity! First, a turbine converts the energy of the moving water into mechanical energy. Then a generator turns that into electrical energy, and transmission lines bring the energy wherever it needs to go.

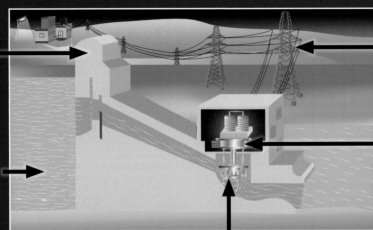

DAM
Raises river level, creating drop of water

RESERVOIR
Stores water

TRANSMISSION LINES
Carry electricity to homes and businesses

GENERATOR
Turned by the turbine, producing electrical energy

TURBINE
Turned by the force of falling water

WORDS TO KNOW

TURBINE
A machine with a wheel or rotor designed to revolve as water or gas passes through it.

GENERATOR
A generator converts mechanical energy into electricity by forcing electric charges in wires to move through an electric circuit.

サン　フランシーキョー

WHY CAN'T YOU DIG STRAIGHT THROUGH THE EARTH?

Fred is digging a trap for Ned, the hermit who lives in Muirahara Woods to avoid all things "techno-illogical." Fred can only dig so far, though. Even if he digged all the way through the Earth's crust, which is more than 110,000 feet thick, he would eventually hit magma! That's because the Earth isn't entirely made from dirt—in fact, it's not even mostly made up of dirt! Our planet is made up of four different layers:

1. INNER CORE
The inner core is in the center. It's solid and made of iron and nickel. It's also incredibly hot, reaching temperatures of up to 5,500 degrees Celcius.

2. OUTER CORE
The outer core is also iron and nickel. But instead of being solid, like the inner core, the outer core is liquid.

3. MANTLE
The mantle is the largest section. It's made up of semi-molten rock called magma.

4. CRUST
The crust, the solid layer of rock and dirt which we live on, is the outer layer of the Earth.

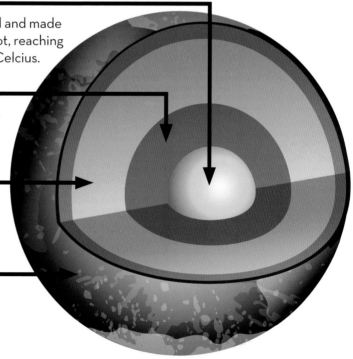

WHY DO WHIRLPOOLS HAPPEN?

KREIFISHER

When Alistair Krei's boat gets stuck in a whirlpool (a swirling body of water), it's because the Mad Jacks caused a tidal wave. But usually whirlpools form because ocean currents traveling in opposite directions meet, creating a vortex in the water. Krei was lucky Hiro and Baymax came to help—getting sucked into a whirlpool can be dangerous!

WHY DO OCEAN CURRENTS MOVE IN DIFFERENT DIRECTIONS?

Unlike river currents, which are controlled by gravity, ocean currents are largely created by wind. Ocean currents can also be affected by tides and temperature. Warm water is less dense than cold water, so when the two meet, the warm water moves so it can float on top of the cooler water.

サン　フランシスキョー

WORDS TO KNOW

VORTEX
A mass of whirling fluid or air.

TIDE
The rising and falling of the ocean. The tides rise and fall because of gravitational pulls from the Earth, moon and sun.

WHY DOES WIND BLOW?

When Fred's kaiju blows air, it really causes some crazy winds! Of course, winds aren't usually caused by giant mutant lizards. Wind is actually caused by the sun! As the sun's light touches the Earth's surface and is converted into heat energy, the atmosphere gets warmer, too. Areas of the Earth that always receive direct sunlight are always at warmer temperatures. Warm air in these areas is less dense than cooler air, causing the warm air to move and flow over the cooler air. This movement is what's happening when we feel the wind blowing.

HOW DO WE TURN WIND INTO ENERGY?

Just like hydroelectric plants in water, windmills and wind turbines convert wind into electricity! The wind turns the blades, creating mechanical energy that powers a generator. The generator produces electricity.

GENERATOR

BLADES

WHY ARE CLOUDS WHITE?

When Hiro has inventor's block, he tries to clear his mind by imagining himself on a fluffy, white cloud. Clouds appear to be white because they are formed by millions of tiny water droplets. Sunlight shining through these clouds scatters all the colors of the visible spectrum: red, orange, yellow, green, blue and violet. When all of those colors are combined, we perceive it as white.

As clouds gather more water droplets and ice crystals, they become much thicker and more dense. This makes it harder for light to penetrate the clouds, so they appear darker.

TYPES OF CLOUDS

Clouds have different names, depending on their altitude and shape.

WHAT'S IN A NAME?
Most cloud names come from Latin words that describe how the cloud appears.

Alto = High
Cirro = Curl
Cumulo = Heap
Nimbus = Rain
Stratus = Layer

CIRRUS
(18,000 feet and higher)

ALTOSTRATUS
(6,000-20,000 feet)

CIRROCUMULUS
(18,000 feet and higher)

ALTOCUMULUS
(6,000-20,000 feet)

STRATOCUMULUS
(6,000 feet or lower)

STRATUS
(6,000 feet or lower)

CUMULUS
(6,000 feet or lower)

CUMULONIMBUS
(Near the ground-50,000 feet)

WHY DOES IT GET FOGGY OUTSIDE?

Hiro and Baymax have a hard time patrolling San Fransokyo when it's foggy out—Hiro can't see anything, and Baymax can't fly as well as he normally can.

Fog is really just clouds that have formed very close to the ground, and clouds are difficult to see through! When warm air meets colder air, water vapor cools down, turning the vapors into tiny water droplets. (The technical word for this process is condensation.) As the area warms up again, the condensation turns back into vapor, and the fog dissipates.

MY FLIGHT FUNCTION IS NOT AT FULL EFFICIENCY IN SUSPENDED WATER DROPLETS.

ACIDIC Any substance with a pH of less than 7.

ANTIBIOTIC A medicine that destroys microorganisms, or keeps them from growing. Antibiotics are often used to treat infections.

ATOMIC NUMBER The number of protons in a nucleus.

BACK UP Archive computer data so it may be restored in the event of a crash.

BASE Any substance with a pH of more than 7.

BIOLUMINESCENCE The creation and release of light by a living organism.

CARTILAGE Firm, white, flexible connective tissue. The human nose and outer ear are made of cartilage.

CEREBELLUM A part of the brain responsible for coordinating and regulating muscle activity.

COMBUSTIBLE A material capable of catching fire and burning.

CONSTANT A component of a scientific experiment that is always the same.

DENSITY A measurement of mass divided by volume, or how much mass is compressed into a certain amount of space. The more dense something is, the more heavy it is by volume.

ENZYME A substance produced by a living organism that causes a certain biochemical reaction.

GENERATOR A generator converts mechanical energy into electricity by forcing electric charges in wires to move through an electric circuit.

HORMONE A chemical substance produced in the body that controls and regulates the activity of certain cells or organs.

HYPOTHESIS A theory made from limited evidence.

KINETIC ENERGY Energy that comes from motion.

LASER Laser stands for Light Amplification by Stimulated Emission of Radiation.

MAGMA Hot, liquid rock.

METABOLISM All the chemical processes in an animal's body. The faster the metabolism, the more energy (food) the animal needs.

MICRON Also known as a micrometer, a micron is a measurement of length one thousandth of a millimeter. One millimeter is equal to .1 centimeters, or about .03 inches.

MOLECULE A group of atoms bonded together. A molecule is the smallest unit of a chemical compound that can take part in a chemical reaction.

MOTOR PROCESSES Activity in the muscles of the body that you can control, also known as "voluntary" activity.

NEUROSCIENTIST A scientist with specialized knowledge of the nervous system, including the brain, spinal cord and nerve cells.

ORBIT The curved path of an object around a star, planet or moon. The Earth orbits around the sun, and the moon orbits around the Earth.

PARASOMNIA Parasomnias are abnormal things that happen while a person sleeps.

PH A measure of hydrogen ion concentration.

PIEZOELECTRIC EFFECT From the Greek piezein, meaning "to squeeze or press," the ability of certain materials to produce an electric charge in response to mechanical stress.

PISTON A disk or short cylinder that fits snugly within a tube. Pistons move up and down against a gas or liquid.

RADIATION The release of energy as electromagnetic waves.

REFRACTION The bending of light as it passes through a substance.

SALIVARY GLAND The glands that produce saliva, salivary glands are located on the inside of each cheek and under the jaw at the front of the mouth and at the bottom of the mouth.

SCALAR QUANTITY A measurement that is only defined by a number, like volume or speed.

STEREOSCOPY A technique for creating the illusion of depth by using binocular (two eye) vision.

TIDE The rise and fall of the ocean. The tides rise and fall because of gravitational pulls from the Earth, moon and sun.

TRILATERATION The process of figuring out a location by using geometry.

TUNED MASS DAMPER A TMD is a vibrating mass that counteracts the motion of the structure to which it is suspended.

TURBINE A machine with a wheel or rotor designed to revolve as water or gas passes through it.

VALENCE ELECTRON An outer shell electron that can form a chemical bond with another element if the outer shell is not already full.

VARIABLE A component of a scientific experiment that changes.

VECTOR QUANTITY A measure that includes a number and a direction, like velocity.

VOLTAGE The pressure that pushes an electrical current through a conducting loop.

VORTEX A mass of whirling fluid or air.

WELD To melt metal pieces and then join them together with pressure.

Media Lab Books
For inquiries, call 646-838-6637

Copyright 2018 Topix Media Lab

Published by Topix Media Lab
14 Wall Street, Suite 4B
New York, NY 10005

Printed in China

ISBN-13: 978-0-9993598-3-9
ISBN-10: 0-9993598-3-5

CEO Tony Romando

Vice President & Publisher Phil Sexton
Senior Vice President Sales & New Markets Tom Mifsud
Vice President of Brand Marketing Joy Bomba
Vice President of Retail Sales & Logistics Linda Greenblatt
Director of Finance Vandana Patel
Manufacturing Director Nancy Puskuldjian
Financial Analyst Matthew Quinn
Brand Marketing Assistant Taylor Hamilton

Editor-in-Chief Jeff Ashworth
Creative Director Steven Charny
Photo Director Dave Weiss
Managing Editor Courtney Kerrigan
Senior Editor Tim Baker

Content Editor Kaytie Norman
Content Designer Rebecca Stone
Content Photo Editor Catherine Armanasco
Art Director Susan Dazzo
Assistant Managing Editor Holland Baker
Senior Designer Michelle Lock
Designer Danielle Santucci
Assistant Photo Editor Stephanie Jones
Assistant Editor Alicia Kort
Copy Editor & Fact Checker Benjamin VanHoose
Editorial Assistants Courtney Henderson-Adams, Sean Romano

Co-Founders Bob Lee, Tony Romando
© 2018 Disney/Pixar

All additonal art and satellite image: Shutterstock.

1C G18 1